THE OAKWOOD PRESS X2

THE GIANT'S CAUSEWAY TRAMWAY

by

J.H. McGuigan

Tram passing the ruins of Dunluce Castle. *Oakwood collection*

THE OAKWOOD PRESS

© J.H. McGuigan, 2007
First Edition 1964
Second Edition 2021
Book redisigned using the original text and photographs added.

ISBN 978-0-85361-756-3

Printed by
Claro Print, Office 26, 27, 1 Spiersbridge Way, Thornliebank, Glasgow G46 8NG

Locomotive No. 4 *Brian Boroimhe*, delivered in 1896 it remained on the tramway until 1931 when it was sold to Mr Faris the contractor building the Bann Breakwater.
Oakwood collection

Front cover: Tram leaves Portrush station for the Giant's Causeway.   *Oakwood collection*

Back cover: Car No. 9 at the Giant's Causeway terminus on 15th April, 1933.
Oakwood collection

Published by
The Oakwood Press, 54-58 Mill Square, Catrine, KA5 6RD
Telephone: 01290 551122   Website: www.stenlake.co.uk

Contents

Preface		5
One	The Pioneering Days	7
Two	Regular Electric Service Commences	23
Three	The Extension Opens	35
Four	A Chapter Of Accidents	41
Five	The 'Trolley' Takes Over	45
Six	The First World War	55
Seven	Motor Charabanc And Omnibus Competition	57
Eight	Difficult Years	65
Nine	Break Downs And Bargains	69
Ten	The Second World War And After	73
Eleven	The Final Years	81

Appendices

One	Steam Locomotives	85
Two	Rolling Stock	87
Three	Walkmills Hydro-Electric Power Station	99
Four	The Overhead System	103
Five	Portrush depot	105
Six	Tickets And Fares	107
Seven	Sentimental Journey	111
Eight	Mr W. A. Traill	117
Index		119

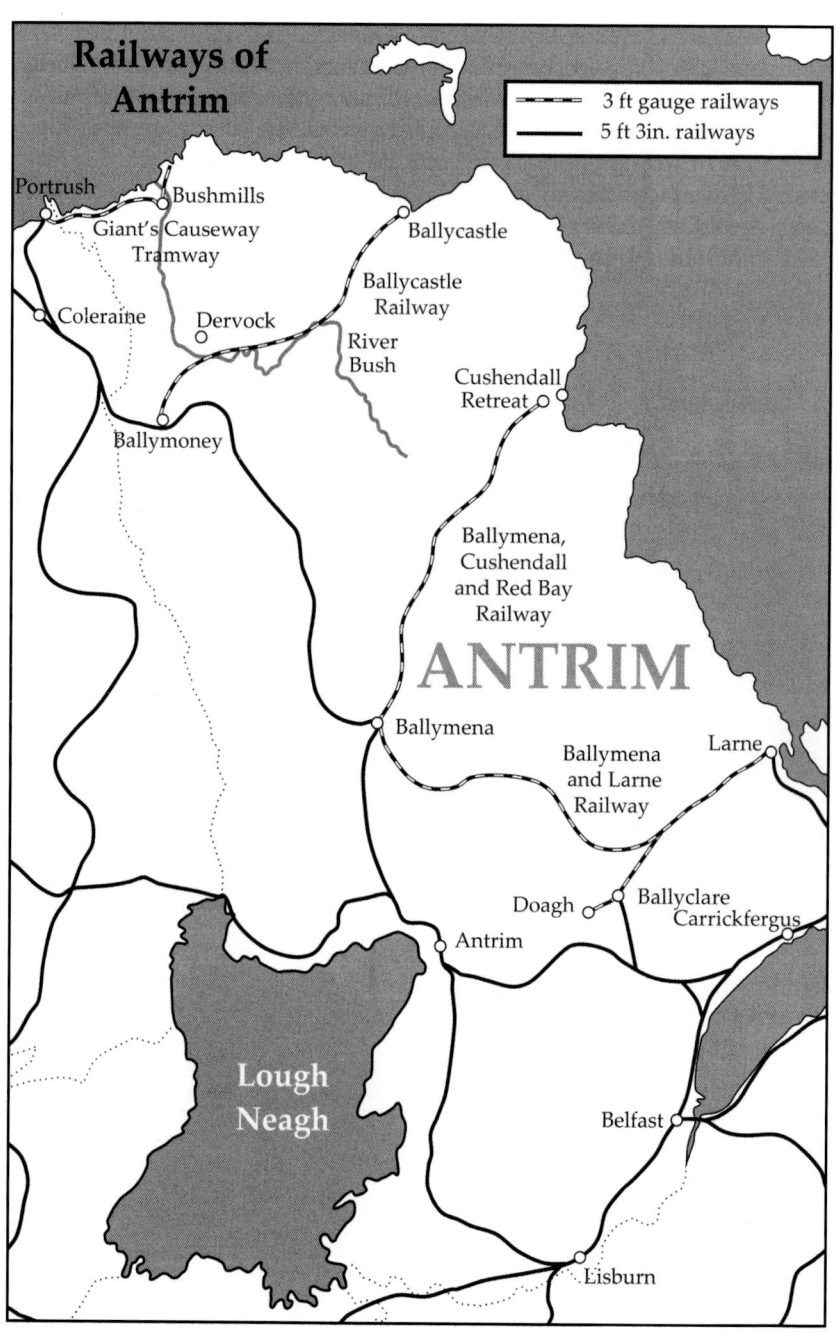

Preface

Some 15 years ago [this preface was written in 1963] I was asked to give a talk to the local area of the Irish Railway Record Society on the subject of the Giant's Causeway Electric Tramway, a line with which I had been familiar from early childhood.

My father came from that part of Co. Antrim, and had personal recollections of the local gossip when the line was opened, and also of its idiosyncrasies during the early years of operation.

Part of our summer holidays were usually spent with relatives in that district, and a much-appreciated treat during these visits was an outing by pony and trap to Bushmills, whence, the pony having been duly and carefully stabled, we travelled on 'the tram' to Portrush. Though I was familiar with the electric trams in Belfast where I lived, the toast-rack cars and 'railway line' track of the Causeway Tram were always a novelty, but the greatest thrill of all was experienced on those occasions when I found our tram headed by one of the Wilkinson steam locomotives. When working hard, the exhaust of these veterans made a noise which can only be likened to that of a runaway traction engine, and they exuded a distinctive aroma compounded of steam, coke fumes, hot oil, and singeing metal, all of which appealed powerfully to the senses of a small boy.

The writing out of the notes for my talk revealed a number of gaps in my information and my curiosity urged me to try to fill them, with a view to preparing a short article on the tramway, which was still working at that time. I commenced operations by chatting to various members of the tram crews, and to the last two managers. The information so gleaned, by enquiry and by personal observation, whetted my thirst for investigation still further, and proved to have initiated a 'snow-ball' reaction, as the cross-checking of known or half-known facts often revealed others long forgotten or hitherto unknown.

This process has continued spasmodically throughout the intervening years, to culminate in this little history of a little, but historic, tramway, which I hope may prove to be interesting and enjoyable reading for the tramway and railway enthusiast.

Information has been gleaned from many sources, and I am grateful to all who have helped in this respect, but I would acknowledge especially the assistance I have received from the following:

Dr. D. B. McNeill, who passed to me notes of his researches into the early history of the tramway; Mr F. G. Stokes Dunbar, Mr S. R. Henry,

Mr M. J. Pollard, and the Public Record Office of Northern Ireland, for kindly granting access to Minute Books and papers relating to the tramway; The Ulster Museum, the Belfast Transport Museum, and the National Library of Ireland, for permission to publish photographs from the Welch and Lawrence Collections; Messrs. C. J. Slator, W. Robb and R. Wilkinson, for loan of photographs; Mrs T. M. Hutchinson, who undertook the typing of the script from somewhat illegible notes; Mr H. Bryans, of the Ulster Museum, for invaluable advice and assistance with the photographic illustrations; and Mr D. G. Coakham, not only for the production of the admirable black and white drawings, but for joining me on numerous enjoyable expeditions to the tramway, when track-layouts were mapped, and dimensions of rolling-stock, etc., measured and recorded.

J. H. MCGUIGAN.
Belfast, June, 1963.

Portrush station about 1910. Steam locomotive No. 4 is in the background motor car No. 23, on the left and No. 9 on the inside line.

National Library of Ireland W. Lawrence collection

Chapter One

The Pioneering Days

Unlike her sister isle Great Britain, Ireland was poorly provided by nature with deposits of coal and iron, though ironically enough, tradition has it that the use of coal as a fuel originated at Fair Head in the north of Antrim, where coal-mining by means of adits driven into the side of the cliff, has been carried on for some hundreds of years, and continues at the present time.

In 1866, a Mr Fisher who had been connected with iron-mining in Cumberland, commenced iron-mining at Glenravel in the north-east of County Antrim, and this initiated a mild 'iron rush' in the district. To provide cheap transport of the ore from mines located at the head of Glenariff, a railway four miles long was constructed down the glen to the sea-coast where a harbour with loading chutes was built. The line was opened in 1873 and the gauge was 3 ft. Why this gauge was chosen is not known, but the favourable report on the gauge by Mr Vignoles, who recommended its adoption for the Isle of Man Railway then under construction, may have had some influence. The interesting point is that it was the first railway in Ireland to be constructed to this gauge and therefore may be credited with initiating what came to be the second 'standard' gauge in Ireland.

Within the next seven years, 60 miles of 3 ft gauge railways had been constructed in County Antrim, viz.: Ballymena to Parkmore and Retreat, 16½ miles; Ballymena to Larne, 25½ miles; and Ballymoney to Ballycastle, 16½ miles. The first two of these undertakings were primarily intended to provide cheap transport for iron ore from the several mines to the port of Larne direct, or via the 5 ft 3 in. gauge Belfast & Northern Counties Railway (BNCR) from Ballymena to the port of Belfast, but the small towns and villages along the line also benefited by the cheap and convenient passenger and goods services provided.

Small communities not on the railways already constructed were inspired to agitate for similar facilities and amongst these was the village of Bushmills, situated about six miles from the well-known seaside resort of Portrush on the north Antrim coast. The Ballymena, Ballymoney, Coleraine, and Portrush Junction Railway had reached Portrush in 1855, and since then it and its successor, the Belfast & Northern Counties Railway, had several times contemplated extending the line via Bushmills to the Giant's Causeway, that well-known geological curiosity and tourist attraction. The cost of constructing a broad gauge line, which would have entailed heavy tunnelling or

A map dated 1879 showing the Giant's Causeway and surrounding lines. Probably the one exhibited by Mr Traill at meetings in 1879.

cutting through basalt, was considered to be prohibitive and nothing was done.

In 1878 a concession was granted by the Grand Jury (the forerunner of the County Council) to a Company, the Ulster Steam Tramway Company, to construct within two years a tramway along the public road from Portrush to Bushmills. This company failed to get any support due to certain dubious financial provisions on the part of the professional promoters.

In 1879, another professional company promoter, alleging that he had bought the concession from the original holders, proceeded in his turn to solicit financial support for the scheme. His efforts met with little more success than those of his predecessors and in 1880 the company was adjudged bankrupt on the petition of a printer to whom it owed £200 19s. 10d. for printing and stationery. From the report of the hearing emerged the interesting information that the promoter of the company was an undischarged bankrupt, that the secretary, who bore the not unusual name of Jones, was in fact the promoter's clerk, and that Mr Jones had recently changed his abode, omitting, doubtless in a moment of absent-mindedness, to mention his new address!

While the wily officials of the Ulster Steam Tramway Company were endeavouring unsuccessfully to augment their personal finances at the expense of the residents of the district, and were discovering that the Ulster Scot was just as strongly attached to his hard-earned bawbees as his cousin across the North Channel, two brothers, Dr. Anthony Traill, Fellow of Trinity College, Dublin, and Mr William Atcheson Traill, M.A. (Ing.), members of a well-known local family, decided to take action in the matter.

Mr W. A. Traill, having been employed for some time in H. M. Geological Survey of Ireland, was understandably interested in the development of the mineral resources of the district, as well as in providing it with a transport system. At a public meeting held on 27th October, 1879 in Bushmills Courthouse to consider the best means by which railway communication for Bushmills could be obtained, Dr. Anthony Traill was the chairman, and a number of the local landowners were present. During the meeting, Mr Wm. Traill displayed a large map of County Antrim on which he had shown the then existing and proposed railway systems in the county, together with the known mineral deposits. He had also shown on the map, the routes of the lines which he and his brother considered to be the best for serving Bushmills. These were, firstly a railway just over nine miles long, from a junction with the Ballymoney–Ballycastle Railway, then approaching

Special Report upon the Minerals and other Economic Products.

Sirs,

Iron Ore. Extensive deposits of Pisolitic Iron Ore (red Hematite), and Bauxite, occur contiguous to the proposed Railway and Tramway. Mines have been opened at Port Moon, Drumnagessan, and at Orblereigh near "The Kennel," but owing to the expense of carting the Ore to port the output has been very limited in amount. Short Branch Tramways would readily connect these mines directly with the Portrush Tramway.

Limestone. Along the Line of Tramway and adjacent to it White Limestone occurs most abundantly ; it is well adapted for agricultural, building, and chemical purposes. Large quarries are now worked at Ballymagarry and a large inland traffic might be expected in addition to that for e$_x$port. Along the Scotch coast there is almost an unlimited demand for this White Limestone for chemical purposes.

Sand. Extensive Sandhills are in the immediate neighbourhood of the Tramway, and the Sand being free from saline matter is well suited for building purposes. as also the Shell Sand for Agriculture.

Seaweed. By a well-directed system of collecting the Sea-weed, as a manure, a large inland trade might be developed.

Salmon. The well-known Salmon fisheries of the river Bush and sea fishery adjacent would be considerably extended, and afford considerable traffic.

W. A. TRAILL, C.E , H.M. Geological Survey.
September 30th, 1879.

Geological survey report by W.A. Traill that was included in the prospectus for the Giant's Causeway Tramway. Author's collection

completion, at a point near Dervock station, thence along the valley of the Bush River to Bushmills, and on to a terminus at the Giant's Causeway and secondly, a tramway just over six miles in length from the Belfast & Northern Counties Railway (BNCR) station in Portrush, along the public road to Bushmills, where a junction would be made with the proposed railway. Both the railway and the tramway would be constructed to the 3 ft gauge already adopted by the Ballycastle Railway, so that through running from Ballymoney and Ballycastle to the Giant's Causeway would be possible. Furthermore, if, as it was confidently expected, a connecting line from a point near Rathkenny on the existing Ballymena & Parkmore Railway to a point between Dervock and Stranocum on the Ballymoney & Ballycastle Railway was built via Cloughmills and Lissanoure, the Giant's Causeway would be brought within 48 miles of Larne by continuous narrow-gauge railway instead of 85 miles by the then existing 5 ft 3 in. gauge Belfast & Northern Counties Railway line to Portrush, and by road thence to the Causeway.

Emphasis was laid on the fact that due to the configuration of the land through which the Dervock–Bushmills–Causeway line would pass, earthworks would be negligible, and the cost of the railway would be correspondingly low, £2,200 per mile being the figure quoted. Only 11 county road bridges or crossings would be required. Stations would be provided at Dervock, Benvarden, Bushmills, and the Giant's Causeway. Mr Traill also pointed out as potential sources of revenue the deposits of iron ore, gravel and sand, and quarries of basalt and limestone which existed and were being worked in close proximity to the route of the proposed railway and tramway, and which only awaited the cheap and convenient transport which would be provided by these undertakings, to expand operations. Agriculture was not forgotten, as Mr Traill pointed out that 'by a well-directed system of collecting seaweed as manure a large import trade might be developed'. Presumably 'import' was used here to mean from the coast inwards to the land, in contrast to the flow of the mineral traffic which would be mostly in the opposite direction.

Tourist traffic to the Causeway, and the salmon fishery on the River Bush and adjacent coast, were also expected to furnish an acceptable addition to the passenger and goods receipts.

After some speeches, and promises from landowners through whose territory the railway would pass, that they would accept shares in the Company as payment for such lands, several resolutions supporting the proposals were passed, and a committee was appointed to go further into the matter.

The Traill brothers went ahead with their plans and the Parliamentary Notice for the Dervock & Giant's Causeway Railway and the Portrush & Bushmills Tramway, duly appeared in the newspapers of November 1879. The Bill was before Parliament in July 1880, when, understandably, it was opposed by Sir W. T. Macnaghten because the Bushmills–Giant's Causeway section of the railway was to pass not only through his demesne, but across the main drive to his residence, Dundarave. He withdrew his opposition when the promoters dropped this section of line from their Bill, which received the Royal Assent on the 28th August, 1880. This Act authorized the construction of

> a Railway 7 miles 1 furlong and 5 chains in length, commencing at or near a point in field Number 11 on the Deposited Plans for the Ballycastle Railway and 4 miles 4 furlongs and 1 chain from the commencement of that Railway

and terminating

> at or near a point on the eastern fence of the public road from Bushmills to the Giant's Causeway, 700 ft or thereabout from the South Pier of the lodge gate of the front avenue of Dundarave House, measured along the fence in a southerly direction.

Also a tramway (Number 1)

> six miles long commencing in the town of Bushmills by a junction with the proposed railway at or near a point in the centre of a field belonging to, or reputed to belong to, and occupied by Sir Francis Macnaghten, Bart., nine hundred feet or thereabout from the point of termination of the railway, and terminating in the town of Portrush at or near a point in the Main Street, fifty feet or thereabout from the north-east corner of the school house, measured in a north-easterly direction.

Also a tramway (Number 4),

> single line, 1 chain 10 links in length commencing in the town of Bushmills by a junction with Tramway Number 1, at or near a point in the centre of the roadway, 30 ft or thereabout from the west front of the clock tower of the Market House, measured in a westerly direction and terminating at the gate entrance of the market place.

Also a tramway (Number 5),

> single line, 1 furlong 8 chains in length, commencing by a junction with Tramway Number 1at its point of termination, and terminating at or near a point in the public road from Portrush to Coleraine, 18 chains or thereabout from the commencement of Tramway Number 5.

Tramways Numbers 2 and 3 were merely passing loops at Dunluce and the Whiterocks.

It will be noted that tramways Numbers 1 and 5 were for a line which passed along the Main Street of Portrush and then turned back to the Portrush–Coleraine Road. This was the route proposed by the Ulster Steam Tramway Company, and the Traills retained it for the purpose of their Bill, to avoid opposition from the Belfast & Northern Counties Railway, but once the Act was obtained, the route was varied to avoid Main Street by turning directly into Eglinton Street, the beginning of the Portrush–Coleraine Road.

An interesting piece of information contained in the Act is the fact that among the original directors of the tramway company was Mr James Chaine, the principal figure behind the Ballymena and Larne narrow-gauge line.

The Act granted the promoters authority to work the said railway and tramway by animal, mechanical, or electrical power, and stipulated that the tramway between Bushmills and Portrush should be completed within two years, five years being allowed for the completion of the railway between Bushmills and Dervock.

Having obtained their Act in the face of active opposition on the part of the Grand Jury, local councils, landlords, and railway companies, and of actual hostility in some instances, from the inhabitants of Portrush and Bushmills, the brothers Traill next found difficulty in raising the capital necessary for the tramway between the latter towns, though they got wide and favourable publicity for their schemes in the local press as well as in the national technical press. Public meetings held in Portrush and Bushmills on 27th and 28th September, 1880 were fully reported, and a number of local gentlemen subscribed for moderate numbers of shares in the undertaking, but it was only due to the help of their friends and acquaintances at Trinity College, Dublin, that the Traills obtained the £20,000 required for this section of the line.

Among the original shareholders were Judge Longfield (£1,000) and Sir Wm. Thompson, later Lord Kelvin (£1,000). Having been approached by Mr Traill, who pointed out the suitability of the line for electrical operation due to the water power readily available at Bushmills, Dr. Wm. Siemens joined the board of directors and took shares amounting to £3,500.

As prior to the introduction of their Bill to Parliament, only one or two short lines in exhibition grounds had been operated electrically, the Traills had shown commendable initiative and foresight in seeking authority to work their line by the new power.

Sufficient capital to commence work having been raised, the first sod was cut with some ceremony, about half a mile from Portrush, by Mrs W. A. Traill on 21th September, 1881, and Dr. Jellett, Provost of Trinity College, Dublin, addressed the gathering. Work was pushed ahead under the direction of Mr W. A. Traill who was the engineer of the Company. The roadway between Portrush and Bushmills had to be widened throughout its length to accommodate the tramway, the track of which was laid at the side of the roadway and at a level slightly above the road surface.

Messrs. Siemens Bros., Queen Anne's Gate, London, had been appointed as the Company's electrical engineers, so as soon as a reasonable length of track had been completed, experiments in electric traction were commenced under the direction of Dr. Edward Hopkinson, Messrs. Siemens Bros.' representative on the site.

As the short electric railways previously constructed in various Exhibition grounds, and the 1½ mile long line at Lichterfelde in Germany, had all been operated on the 'Two-rail' system, the first experiments on the Portrush line were carried out on this system, in which the track rails were insulated from each other and were used as the positive and negative conductors. The tramcar wheels were of wood with iron tyres, to prevent short circuiting via the wheels and axles of the cars.

For these experiments, a Siemens dynamo driven by a 25 horse power agricultural type stationary steam engine was installed in the depot building at Portrush. The dynamo had an output of 15 kilowatts at 250 volts.

Experiments carried out over a period of several months showed that, whilst the two-rail system operated reasonably well in dry weather, in wet weather the cars could not be operated more than about two miles distant from the power station, due to the excessive current leakage between the rails. An attempt was made to improve the insulation between the rails, by laying them in asphalt on top of a thick layer of felt without achieving any notable success, and it was then decided to experiment with the third-rail system. As the tramway ran along the side of the public road, the most suitable position for the third rail was obviously between the track and the hedge where it was less liable to damage, and also less likely to be the cause of accident to other road users.

The conductor rail adopted was of 'T' section wrought-iron, weighing 19 lb. per yard, and in 21 ft lengths. Each joint was made with two fish-plates, and two copper bonds which were securely soldered to the ends of the iron rails, as it was found that the fish-plates alone gave rather

Motor-car No.4 and trailer (probably No. 10) at Bushmills. Note current collectors at each end of the motor-car and also at the rear of the trailer. *Author's collection*

uncertain continuity. Similar copper bonds were fitted at each joint in the track rails as these of course provided the return circuit. The conductor rail was supported on wooden posts which were driven into the ground alongside the hedge at 10 ft intervals and which were so arranged that the conductor rail was 22 in. from the inside running rail and 17 in. above track level.

Each post was boiled in pitch to impart a degree of waterproofing and the top was notched to receive the web of the 'T' iron conductor, the top of the post being coated with tar before the conductor was placed in position.

A metal brush supported on a steel arm projecting from the side of the motor car served to collect current from the conductor rail, the circuit to the power station being completed via the axle-boxes, wheels, and running rails.

With this system a fair degree of success was achieved, though in wet weather the leakage current was still much too high, and experiments were carried out to try and improve matters by fitting insulators of various materials between the conductor rail and the tops of the supporting posts. The final choice at that time was the (then) recently invented material 'Insulite' formed by forcing paraffin wax at very high pressure into sawdust. When insulators of this material were fitted, a resistance of from 500 ohms to 1,000 ohms per mile was obtained, depending on atmospheric conditions. Eventually moulded porcelain inserts were found to be most satisfactory. Where side roads or field entrances occurred, the conductor rail had, of course, to be interrupted, and continuity at such points was maintained by bridging the gap with a suitable length of insulated copper cable carried through a length of wrought-iron tubing laid 18 in. below the surface of the ground.

By fitting a collecting brush at each end of the motor car, current was not interrupted in passing gaps of between 16 ft and 18 ft. Where gaps exceeding this length occurred, the momentum of the car was sufficient to carry it across the gap. Later on, when trailer cars were in regular use, a collector brush was fitted on the trailer and connected to the motor car by flexible cable, thus permitting gaps of roughly 35 ft to be negotiated under power.

By the end of 1882, the track from Portrush station to Bushmills Market Yard had been completed, together with a branch to Portrush harbour, which was constructed by laying a third rail along the BNCR's 5 ft 3 in. gauge harbour branch, to accommodate the 3 ft gauge tramway vehicles. From Portrush depot to the railway station, and for the last quarter mile to Bushmills Market Yard, the track was laid on the carriage-way. As it was obvious that the elevated conductor rail could not be installed along the line where it passed through the streets of Portrush and Bushmills, two steam tramway locomotives were ordered from Messrs. Wilkinson & Co. of Wigan, to work the trams along these sections, and also to work the goods and mineral traffic which was confidently expected to develop.

On 12th January, 1883 the line was inspected by Major-General Hutchinson, the Board of Trade's Inspector of Railways. One of the two steam locomotives, which had been delivered a few days previously, and an open car, were used for the inspection, which included a visit to the car shed and electrical generating plant at Portrush, and the General expressed himself as highly pleased with the way in which the work had been carried out. The party which numbered about 10 persons, including Mr Tate, the County Surveyor, then made a short trip on the electric car, Mr Traill acting as driver. This also met with general approval though the amount of sparking at the rails called forth considerable comment.

Official approval having been received from the Board of Trade, the line was opened for public traffic on 29th January, 1883, the two steam locomotives of course, being used to handle the trains pending completion of the electrical experiments. Early in February Mr Traill stated that the total cost of construction had been £21,000. The rolling stock at the time of the Board of Trade inspection in January 1883 was given as: 2 Wilkinson steam locomotives, 2 open first-class cars with motors, 2 closed first-class cars, 3 open third-class cars, and goods wagons (number unspecified), all of which, except the steam locomotives, had been constructed by the Midland Carriage & Wagon Company. There was also an unspecified number of tipping wagons on Geoghegan's Patent, built by Messrs. Ross & Walpole of Dublin. Mr Geoghegan, was engineer at Guinness' Brewery in Dublin.

It was hoped to have electrification completed and the line officially opened by the Lord Lieutenant in the spring, but a lawsuit over water rights between the Land Commission and the farmer on whose land it was proposed to erect the hydro-electric station, was only settled at the latter end of February, so that it was the month of March before the Company could get their legal agreement on water rights, etc., completed and commence work on the station.

The site works involved the construction of a channel 9 ft wide, 8 ft deep, and 200 yards long to bring the water of the River Bush from the upper level to the point at Walkmills where the river dropped steeply in a series of rapids and at which it was proposed to erect the station.

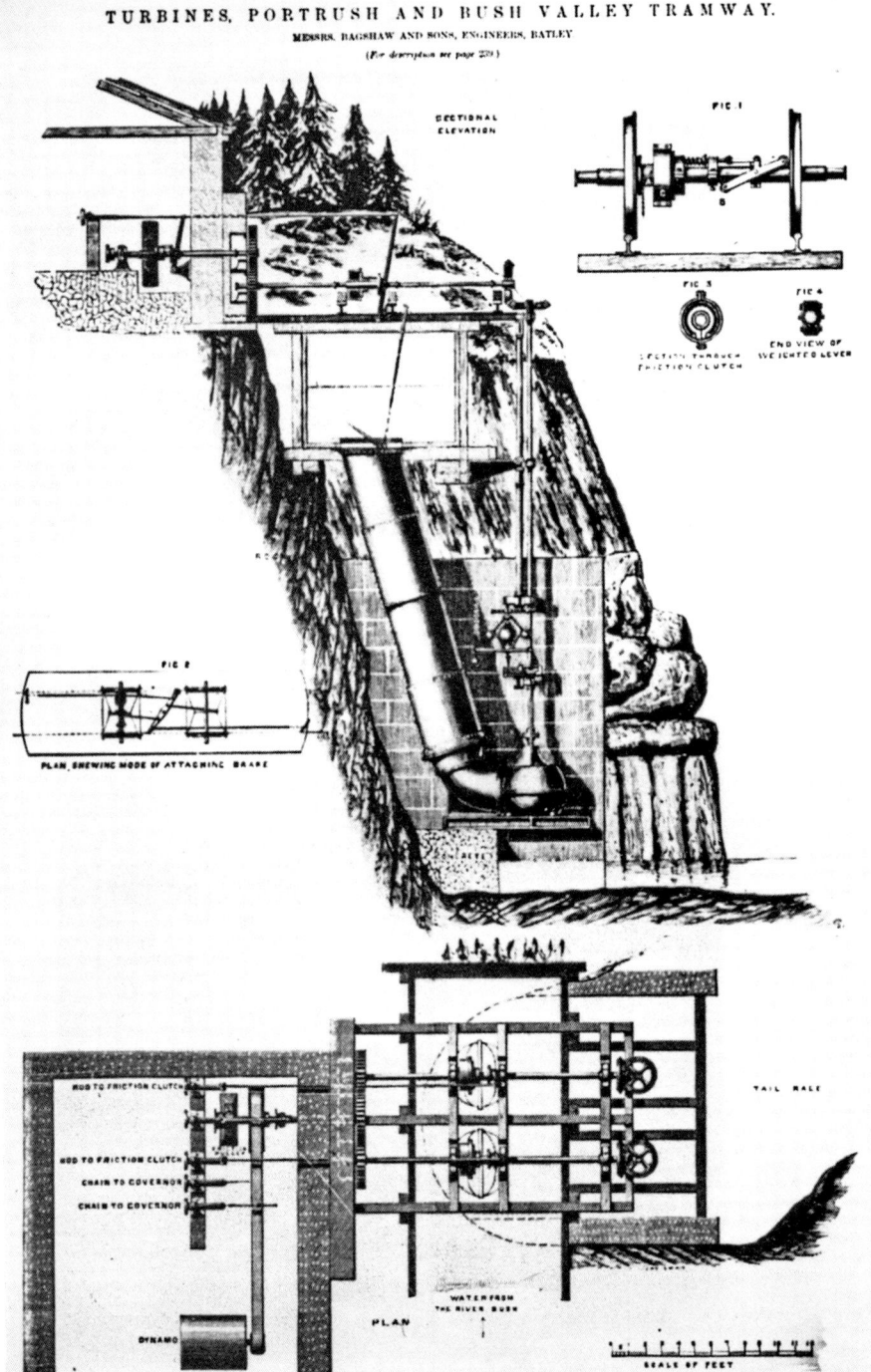

A cross-section of the Walkmills Power Station from *The Engineer* 28th September, 1883. The inset drawings show Price's patent speed limiting device for the cars.

Author's collection

An old flax mill on the site had to be blown up, and extensive rock blasting had to be carried out to prepare a recess in the cliff face to accommodate the penstocks and turbines, and to form a tail race in the river bottom. All these works, together with the building of the house for the dynamos and the construction of an access roadway, were carried out under the personal supervision of Mr W. A. Traill. A contemporary report stated that 'the whole aspect of the place is much beautified' by these works.

On 24th March, the Company applied to the Grand Jury for permission to construct a branch approximately 1¾ miles long to Orblereagh Mines, about a mile south of Portrush, but the application was put back to the Summer Assizes, and was, in fact, refused in July.

Whilst demolition and construction were proceeding at Walkmills, the steam tram locomotives were maintaining a regular service on the line, but on 16th April one of the steam locomotives burst a boiler tube and came to a stop on the line. The generator at Portrush was started up and the electric car went out and towed the crippled engine back to Portrush, surely the first occasion on which a steam locomotive was rendered assistance by an electric locomotive. Passengers arriving at Portrush by the evening train were conveyed by the electric car to the Whiterocks, and thence by jaunting car to Bushmills. Why the passengers were only conveyed as far as the Whiterocks in the electric car is a bit of a mystery as the account of the incident was accompanied by the statement that 'the Electric Car is now frequently seen on the line and it is able to run as far as Dunluce, a distance of four miles.' Possibly the incident occurred on a wet day when the insulation of the conductor rail was not at its best!

The Company's Time-table commencing 1st May, 1883 showed seven trams in each direction, beginning with the 7.20 am from Portrush and

	Ordinary Car		First Class			
	Single	Return	Single	Return		
Portrush–Bushmills	6d.	1s.	1s.	1s. 6d.		
Portrush–Causeway	1s.	2s.	1s. 6d.	2s. 6d.		
Short journey tickets	3d.	—	6d.	—		
Combined	Ordinary Car		First Class		Second Class	
Tram and Rail	Single	Return	Single	Return	Single	Return
Bushmills–Coleraine	1s.	1s. 9d.	2s.	3s.	1s. 9d.	2s. 6d.

Fares quoted in the first timetable.

finishing with the 7.30 pm from Bushmills. Two trams from Portrush and one from Bushmills were noted as ones for which the Company accepted no responsibility for keeping to time-table, and therefore probably indicated mixed goods and passenger trains. Jaunting cars maintained connection between Bushmills and the Causeway Hotel.

It was also stated that on certain days during May and June the electric car would make special excursion trips starting from the tramway depot, Portrush, fare 1s., the times of these excursions to be advertised from time to time in the press.

In a paper describing the tramway which was read before the Society of Arts in London on 11th April, 1883, Dr. Hopkinson stated that at that time only one car had been fitted with 'a dynamo' (motor) but four other dynamos were on order from Messrs. Siemens and it was therefore hoped to have five motor cars, two of which would each be capable of pulling a trailer, available in time for 'the heavy summer traffic'. The paper also included calculations to prove that a motor of 5 h.p. was adequate to propel a tramcar with 20 passengers and having a gross weight of 4 tons, up a gradient of 1 in 37. Presumably the original motors were of this power.

The hope that the summer traffic would be handled by the electric cars was not realized for, while the cars themselves may have been ready, the hydro-electric plant at Walkmills was not, as it was reported about the middle of August that the electric cars could run the six miles from Portrush to Bushmills worked by the small stationary steam engine and generator at Portrush, but it was hoped to have 'the great power to be developed from the Bushmills generator' available before the official opening which was fixed for 14th September. The report also mentioned that on 14th August three wagon loads of machinery for Bushmills had been loaded at Portrush from the Morecambe steamer.

Though the engineer reported to the half-yearly meeting of the directors held on 20th August, that the hydro-electric station at Bushmills would be ready before 14th September, for some reason the official opening ceremony was postponed till 28th September.

In view of the importance attached to the occasion by the Traill brothers (invitations to be present at the ceremony had been sent to every eminent personage in Europe including Queen Victoria, the Emperor of Germany, and other crowned heads), the toil and sweat expended in getting the plant ready, the anxiety when some part of the equipment developed an apparent defect and the relief when the defect was put to rights, which prevailed during the weeks immediately preceding the official opening can well be imagined.

The opening ceremony by the Lord Lieutenant of Ireland, John Poyntz Spencer, 5th Earl Spencer on 5th September, 1883. *Oakwood collection*

At last the great day dawned, 28th September, 1883. The Lord Lieutenant, Earl Spencer, who had been the overnight guest of Sir Hervey Bruce at Downhill, arrived by special train at the BNCR station, Portrush, at ten minutes after noon. The Viceregal party then entered 'the two handsome saloon tramcars of the Tramway Company' which, drawn by one of Messrs. Wilkinson's steam locomotives and accompanied by a mounted escort of the Royal Irish Constabulary, proceeded through the streets of Portrush to the tram depot, where the party alighted and inspected the car sheds and steam-driven generating plant. The Viceregal party then took their seats in the first of the three electric cars.

> a handsome first-class open car, identical to the first-class saloon cars, but having a light canopy overhead instead of the fixed roof upon the covered cars.

Under the guidance of Mr W. A. Traill, His Excellency performed the ceremony of operating the handles to start the car on its journey; for the remainder of which it was driven by Mr W. A. Traill in person, and arrived safely at Bushmills in about half an hour. It was followed by the other two electric cars, each carrying about 20 persons. One of the steam locomotives with a train of cars containing about 100 of the less distinguished guests in the party brought up the rear, and probably also acted as a last line of defence in case the temperamental electrical equipment should decide to sulk.

The party having arrived safely at Bushmills, the Lord Lieutenant made a short speech in which he declared the line open. He then entered Dr. Traill's private carriage and, again attended by a mounted escort of the Royal Irish Constabulary, was driven to the hydro-electric station at Walkmills, where the party assembled to inspect the plant and, quoting, 'the several beautiful instruments for testing the electric currents and the resistances along the line, which together with the switch boxes for putting on and cutting off the current, are all in their proper places.' There was also the telephone by which communication was maintained between the hydro-electric station and the depots at Portrush and Bushmills, and which utilized the same conductors as those used to transmit the power to the tramway.

During the visit to the power station, Sir William Thompson (later Lord Kelvin) entertained those present, and at the same time demonstrated the 'Perfect safety' [sic] of the 250 volt supply, by shaking hands with unsuspecting members of the party, whilst he unobtrusively held the unearthed terminal of the dynamo with his other hand, thus subjecting those so favoured to an unexpected, but doubtless beneficial, shock treatment.

The perpetration of this prank by Sir William is an indication of the state of electrical knowledge in 1883, as no present-day engineer or scientist in his right mind would expose random individuals to a voltage of this order.

The supply of victims for Sir William's little joke having become exhausted, and having gazed their fill at the scientific wonders on view, the party again took carriages, and the Viceregal party at least, repaired to Ballylough House, the residence of Dr. Traill, who had recently been appointed High Sheriff of County Antrim, where they partook of a 'luncheon-dejeuner'.

During his after-luncheon speech, Dr. Traill stated that since the line was opened 'on 1st February' the weekly receipts had been as follows: February, £11; March, £,18; April, £18; May, £36; June, £50; July, £87; August, £103; the total receipts for the first half of the year being £600, and for the 12 weeks commencing 1st July £,1,077. He went on to state that if the electrical arrangements had been completed earlier in the year, the foregoing figures could have been doubled, that an average of £50 per week would cover all expenses and pay a dividend of 5 per cent, that the fare from Portrush to the Causeway and back (between

Bushmills and the Causeway passengers were conveyed by road on horse cars) was 1s. 9d., and that the ordinary fare was 6d. for six miles. He also exhorted any other persons contemplating railway construction to follow the lead of his Company, avoid professional financiers and promoters and construct their line themselves, paying cash for all materials, as by so doing his Company had completed their line for half the cost at which a previous company had proposed to make it, and the line had been better constructed than any of its kind elsewhere.

Mr W. A. Traill, in his speech, mentioned that £25,000 was still required for the line from Bushmills to Dervock, and that this offered a splendid opportunity for investors, or even for the Government, to employ a little capital usefully. History indicates that this appeal fell on deaf ears.

Speeches having been completed, the party travelled by carriage to Bushmills, where they boarded the waiting tramcars, in which they returned to Portrush railway station, from which they departed in a special train.

The auspicious occasion had passed without a hitch so far as the party, the press, and the public were aware. Behind the scenes things were far from tranquil. Just before the Viceroy entered the electric car at Portrush, Mr Traill got a message to say that a leak had developed at an unknown point between the hydroelectric station at Bushmills and Portrush depot. There was no time to trace the fault and effect a repair. The only thing to be done was to start up the small generator at Portrush, and hope for the best. This was done and Mr Traill gave strict instructions, that the second and third electric cars were not to move from the depot until the first car with the Lord Lieutenant had got over the summit of the line. Fortunately this precaution was effective in getting the whole party safely to Bushmills, and while the inspections, junketings, and speeches were progressing, the electrical staff were hunting for the fault, which luckily they were able to locate and repair in time for the return journey. The insulation of one of the lengths of underground cable, used to maintain continuity across one of the numerous field entrances, had broken down. These lengths of cable continued to be a source of trouble throughout their lifetime, cable-making in the early 1880s being largely in the experimental stage.

Presumably a special effort had been made to operate the line electrically for the official opening, and probably temporary expedients had been employed to permit the use of the electric cars on that day, for electrically-operated public services to a regular schedule did not commence until 5th November, 1883.

Chapter Two

Regular Electric Service Commences

Though subsequent portions of this book deal in some detail with power plant, rolling stock, etc., a description of the line and short account of the power station and rolling stock as it existed when regular operation by electric cars commenced, is necessary at this point to permit the reader to follow intelligently the intervening historical narrative.

The tramway consisted of a single track line of 3 ft gauge, laid with steel rails weighing 42 lb. per yard on a raised path 7 ft wide on the seaward side of the main road from the tramway depot on the outskirts of Portrush to the intersection of that road with the road from Portballintrae, on the outskirts of Bushmills, a distance of about 5½ miles.

From Portrush tram depot to Portrush station, a distance of about half a mile, the line was laid as an ordinary street tramway at the side of the carriage way in Causeway Street and Eglinton Street, terminating in a

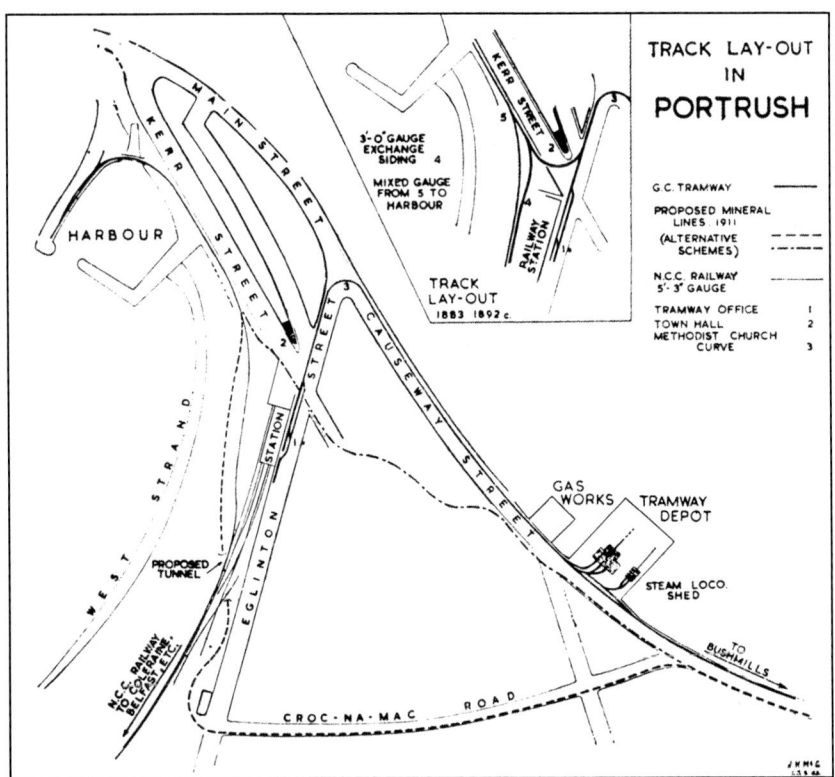

run-round loop and siding alongside the BNCR station. The present railway station with its spacious forecourt had not then been built and the open platforms, enclosed by a masonry wall, extended to the footpath in Kerr Street.

From the corner of Eglinton Street and Mark Street, a branch from the tramway curved round the end of the Town Hall and across Kerr Street to join the harbour branch of the BNCR, along which, as already stated, an additional rail was laid to permit the 3 ft gauge tramway vehicles to run to and from the harbour, with a view to shipping limestone, iron ore, and agricultural produce, and to loading with coal, etc., for the return trip. An exchange siding with the BNCR was taken from the harbour branch.

From the Portballintrae Road at Bushmills, the line was laid as a street tramway on the public road for about 300 yards into the Market Yard.

On account of the elevated conductor rail, electrical operation was restricted to that portion of the line between Portrush depot and Portballintrae Road, Bushmills, the electric cars being hauled by steam tramway locomotives through the streets of Portrush and Bushmills. The steam locomotives also worked the Portrush harbour branch.

Steam locomotive either No.1 or 2 and motor-cars Nos. 4 and 7 at old BNCR station Portrush; behind the crane on the left are limestone tip-wagons. The line of the mixed gauge Harbour branch curves in front of the town hall.
Ulster Museum, R.J. Welch collection

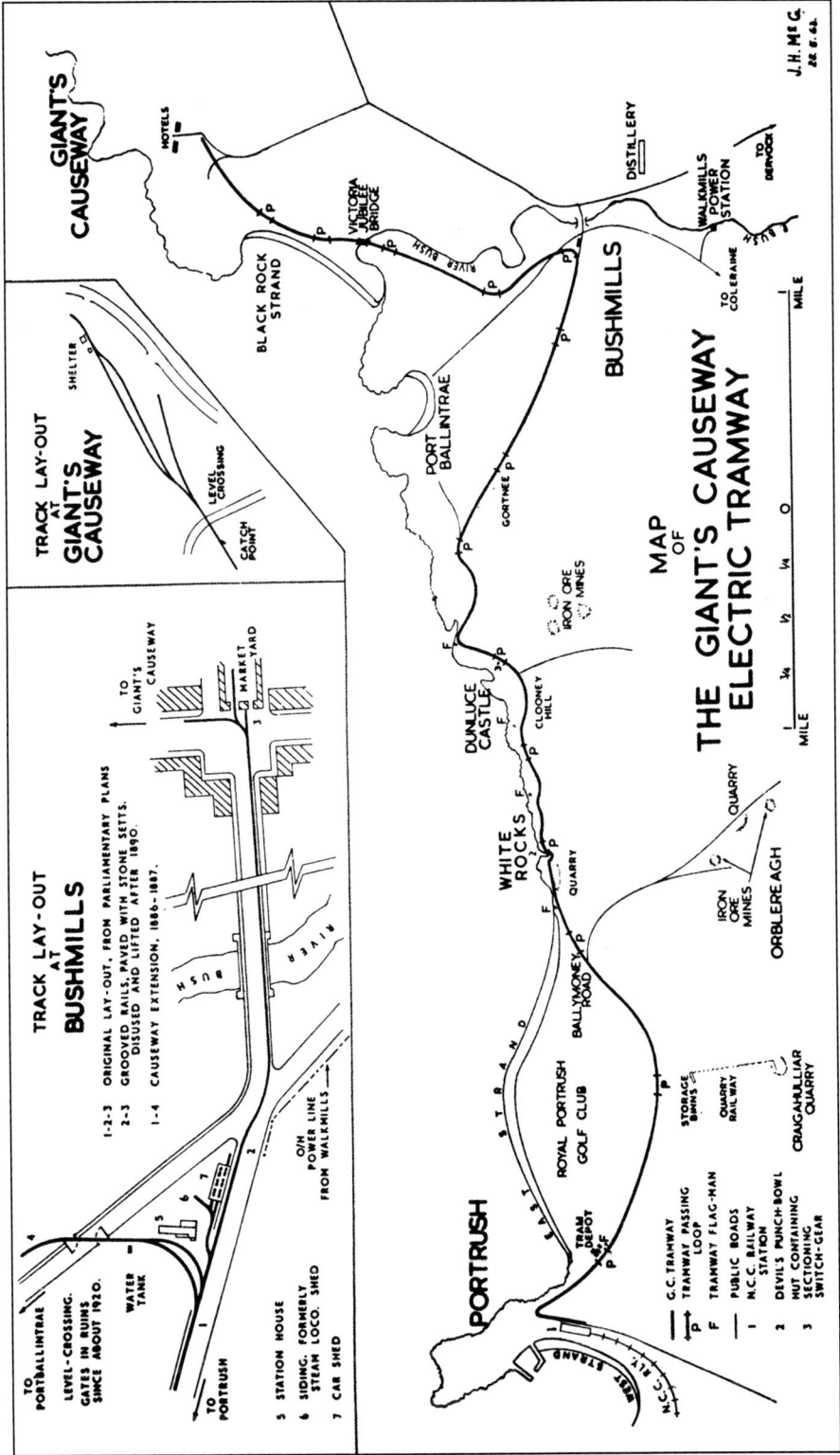

The only known photograph of a goods wagon in use. Locomotive No. 1 or 2 at Portrush depot about 1888.
National Library of Ireland W. Lawrence collection

Although the original plans for the line only allowed for two passing loops between Bushmills and Portrush depot, at Dunluce and at the Whiterocks, five loops had been provided by the time of the opening ceremony, say one every mile. (This number was later increased to eight.) As the conductor rail had to be kept out of the way alongside the hedge, at passing loops the cars going uphill and requiring power kept to the seaward track, whilst cars going downhill used the track next to the roadway. Weighted point levers at the passing loops kept the points set in the appropriate position.

Portrush depot was a not unhandsome building in rough basalt masonry with white brickwork at the corners, around the windows, etc., and was provided with three tracks, each capable of accommodating about four vehicles. A separate running shed of wooden construction was provided for the steam locomotives.

From Portrush railway station the street tramway section was on a falling gradient for about half a mile, to the tram depot, the maximum gradient being 1 in 44 in Causeway Street. From the depot the line climbed gently for about half a mile, and then the gradient gradually steepened to 1 in 40 just before the Ballymoney Road junction was reached, at which point commenced the descent at 1 in 44 past the Whiterocks and Long Gilbert Quarry, beyond which the line again commenced to climb for about a mile at 1 in 40 round the sharp curve at the Devil's Punch Bowl, and the succeeding, but somewhat easier, reverse curves, after which the gradient stiffened to 1 in 33 for a quarter of a mile before reaching the summit of the line, 193 ft above sea-level, at Clooney Hill. From Clooney Hill a descent of about three-quarters of a mile at a gradient of 1 in 35, steepening to 1 in 30 brought the line to the road leading to Dunluce Castle and about 200 yards of more or less level track, before a short climb at 1 in 40 led into a sharp curve round the headland known as the Gallery, at which point there was an almost sheer drop of over 150 ft from the outer edge of the tramway to the sea below. From the Gallery the line descended at 1 in 40 for about a hundred yards and then rose gently to Portballintrae Road. A further descent at about 1 in 40 and a slight climb brought the line to the point from which a foot-path through the fields, known locally as 'the Port Hedge' led directly to the small fishing village of Portballintrae. The tramway then dropped continuously at 1 in 45 and 1 in 50, for 1¼ miles to the Portballintrae Road crossing, where the line crossed the road and ran along the landward side of the carriageway as an ordinary street tramway across the bridge over the River Bush to enter and cross Bushmills Square. The line then turned towards the Causeway Road and ended in a short siding. One branch siding ran into the Market Yard and another stub siding terminated against the wall of the Market Yard.

From the Portballintrae Road, the cable carrying the electricity supply was laid underground for a distance of a little under a mile along the Coleraine Road, to the hydro-electric power station at Walkmills.

The power station was situated about 300 yards from the Coleraine Road, at the Salmon Leap on the River Bush, and was a rectangular building of random masonry in black basalt, about 30 ft long and 25 ft wide.

It housed a bi-polar Siemens dynamo, belt-driven from a countershaft which in turn was driven through a system of gearing by two vertical shaft turbines, each of 45 h.p. giving a total of about 90 h.p.

The rolling stock figures given at the time of the B.o.T. inspection in January 1883 almost certainly held good at the time of the official opening in September. The two first-class saloon cars, and the two first-class open cars had longitudinal seating with cushions, whilst the three open third-class cars were of toast-rack type, each with six cross-bench seats, four passengers to a row, giving 24 seats per car.

Six of the seven original vehicles were still in service when the line ceased working, more than 60 years later.

Detailed descriptions of the power station, locomotives, and rolling stock are given in subsequent chapters.

As already stated, the tramway had been operating from 29th January, 1883 with the two steam locomotives, and in February, within a few days of opening, the board ordered that 'a siding be made into Mr Gray's quarry to the top of the slope, with a back shunt, at a cost not to exceed £85'. This would be the quarry just beyond the Whiterocks, and the rates agreed with Mr Gray were 10d. per ton for coal from Portrush harbour to the quarry and 8d. per ton for limestone from the quarry to the harbour, or 6d. per ton to the BNCR railway siding. The difference of 2d. per ton between carriage to the harbour and to the Northern Counties Railway siding was presumably due to the fact that in October 1882 the tramway company had made an agreement with the Harbour Tramway Company to pay a toll of 2d. per ton on traffic passing over the harbour tramway, with a minimum payment of £50 per annum.

The application in March for the 1¾ mile extension to the iron ore mines at Orblereagh was another effort to foster a mineral traffic.

In the same month an agreement was made with a Mrs Fitzgerald for her 'long cars' to convey passengers from Bushmills to the Giant's Causeway at a charge of 6d. single or 9d. return, 'ticket holders to be accommodated first'. A 'long car' was a four-wheeled version of the Irish 'jaunting car' on which passengers sat back to back, as on the 'knife-board' seats on the upper deck of certain tram cars.

A point which had caused some friction with the local populace was the Company's running of Sunday trams, but by July it was recorded that these services had proved to be more than successful.

At a meeting of the board at the end of July it was stated that through rates for goods between Bushmills and Belfast had been agreed with the BNCR second-class merchandise, 13s. 3d. per ton: sixth class, 45s. per ton; potatoes, 10s. 6d. per ton; grain, 11s. per ton.

An enquiry from the Iron Ore Company for the provision of a siding at Ballymoney Road for iron ore traffic was also considered at the same meeting, presumably as a result of the rejection by the Grand Jury of the application for permission to build the Orblereagh branch. The board ordered that the Mining Company be informed that the siding would be constructed provided that a down payment of £100 towards the cost was forthcoming, and that the rate to the harbour would be 10d. per ton. Presumably the Mining Company was not prepared to make the down payment, as nothing further was done.

In August 1883 the engineer stated that more rolling stock would be required to meet the traffic requirements and the board decided to order as follows: one first-class open electric car, two third-class open cars, one third-class covered car, one composite car, and two goods wagons.

This is the point at which difficulty arises in fixing the dates on which certain vehicles were acquired. As far as can be ascertained, only two first-class open cars ever existed, Nos. 3 and 4, unless some of the toast-rack cars were designated first-class and, possibly, were provided with cushioned seats, but no record of this exists. However, three additional passenger vehicles and two goods wagons had been acquired by the end of 1884 for the rolling stock on 31st December, 1884 was returned as 2 steam locomotives, 4 electric cars, 6 trailers and 14 goods wagons, and the engineer then reported that 'the additional tramcars and wagons ordered have now all been delivered, so they will be available for next season's (1885) running'. This indicates some discrepancy, as the seven passenger vehicles existing at the beginning of 1883, together with the five vehicles 'ordered' in August 1883 would have totalled 12 vehicles, whereas the official returns for the end of 1884 gave a total of only 10 passenger cars. We will leave this mystery for the time being.

In May 1884 the engineer was instructed to proceed with the erection of a shed to hold an engine and two carriages at Bushmills 'at the cross roads where the electric car stops'. In August a Scottish excursionist named Walter White fell off the tram and was seriously injured, the first recorded instance of a passenger being injured on the line.

The Company had by this time acquired an interest in, or at any rate had come to an arrangement with, the Causeway Hotel, for a contemporary advertisement stated that 'the Causeway Hotel is now worked in connection with the Tramway' and exhorted would-be travellers to 'Book through to the Causeway and do not mind false reports by interested persons'- a somewhat cryptic and not altogether reassuring statement.

At the half-yearly general meeting in August, the chairman's remarks included the statement that the electric locomotives had run 9,240 miles, that electricity was very satisfactory though there had been early troubles with it, and that 'the first machines they had were now only fit for museums and they had been sent back to Siemens for modernization'. This is very interesting as showing the rate of development of electrical machines at that period.

At a board meeting in September 1884, it was decided that the engine drivers' wages were to be reduced to 28s. per week, presumably for the winter months. Just before the commencement of public operation in 1883, one William White had been engaged as engine driver at 33s. per week, whilst Howard Moon signed up as conductor at the modest wage of 15s. per week.

CAUSEWAY HOTEL AND ELECTRIC TRAMWAY.

THIS beautifully-situated Hotel is worked in connection with the GIANT'S CAUSEWAY ELECTRIC TRAMWAY. It is the most central spot for Tourists visiting the district, being close to the Giant's Causeway, and with Dunluce Castle, Dunseverick Castle, Ballintoy, and Carrick-a-Rede in the immediate neighbourhood.

The Hotel stands in its own grounds of 40 Acres, and has been greatly enlarged within the last few years to meet the growing popularity of the Establishment, which will be found replete with every comfort. The Hotel is lighted throughout with the Electric Light. There are Asphalte and Grass Lawn Tennis Courts and Golf Links, a German Kiosk, and Electric Holophote.

Guides, Boats, and Posting are attached to the Hotel, with fixed scale of charges.

Electric Tram Cars leave Portrush Station on the arrival of all trains, with through booking to the Causeway Hotel. Tourists are landed in the Hotel grounds without any trouble or change of Cars. There will be an increased service of Electric Tram Cars on the Tramway during the summer months, and the Antrim coast service will be entirely remodelled. Orders to view the Electric Generating Station at Walkmills can be obtained at the Hotel.

Postal and Telegraph Address—The MANAGER, Causeway Hotel, Bushmills.

Note.—Always ask for through Railway Tickets to the Giant's Causeway.

1892 advert for the Giant's Causeway Hotel and lectric Tramway.

Oakwood collection

At the end of 1884, the engineer was ordered to proceed with the erection of an extra shed for carriages and wagons at Portrush. The rolling stock at 31st December, 1884 was given as 2 steam engines, 4 electric cars, 6 trailers, and 14 goods wagons.

Early in 1885 the board met to consider an extension from Bushmills to the Giant's Causeway, for which a Bill was then before Parliament. It was decided to proceed with the above in preference to the line to Dervock, but powers for constructing the latter were to be retained. It was also stated that the Company had an option to purchase the Causeway Hotel.

Later on in the year, the directors authorized the raising of additional capital to finance the Causeway Extension, and the provision of a station at Bushmills.

Incidentally, some of the information elicited during the inquiry into the above Bill, held on 5th, 6th, and 7th May, 1885, was both interesting and entertaining.

Dr. Anthony Traill, having admitted to having been High Sheriff of the County of Antrim in 1882, and to being a Fellow of Trinity College, Dublin, went on to state that the previous company formed under the 1878 Act, had estimated that the tramway from Portrush to Bushmills would cost £30,000. His company had constructed it for £,15,000. The electrical experiments had cost £5,500.

Of the subscribed capital, £890 was held by local residents in small amounts, £7,400 by residents in the district in amounts larger than £200, and £7,600 by scientific men such as Sir Wm. Thompson (later Lord Kelvin), Sir Chas. Siemens, and Sir Frederick Bramwell.

Sir Wm. Thompson, during examination by the Committee, agreed that he had been engaged in electrical science for many years, and had been consulted at all stages of the electrical experiments on the tramway. He was closely questioned on the effect which an electric current at 250 volts would have on human beings and animals. He stated that at that pressure, 'the maximum current which would pass through a human being would be about 1/10 amp or 1/100 of a strong working current'. This quickly brought the question, 'If 500 people all touched the

One of the original steam locomotives pulling a rake of carriages from Portrush terminus. This indicates the variety of carriages owned by the tramway. *Author's collection*

conductor rail simultaneously would the tram be stopped?' Sir William refused to be drawn further than to admit that such a contingency 'would seriously impair the insulation of the line, and diminish the power of the tram'.

Mr W. A. Traill was also examined. Having stated that there was little danger to persons from the live rail, especially as clothing was a fairly good insulator, he was asked would it not be dangerous if a beggar with torn trousers - or a Highlandman sat on it. Mr Traill replied that this very same question had been posed during the B.o.T. inspection of the line prior to its opening, by the inspecting officers, Major General Hutchinson and Major Armstrong. At that time he himself had removed his trousers from the appropriate portion of his anatomy and sat on the live rail, as had Dr. Hopkinson, without any dire result.

Mr Traill stated, furthermore, that far from being dangerous, the shocks received from the live rail were beneficial for rheumatism, and not only himself but other people also, purposely took shocks from the rail with beneficial results. A Portrush doctor sent his patients out to take shocks

Steam locomotive No.4 with five trailers outside Portrush station. Second from the front is motor-car No. 3 which will take over once the third rail is reached and the steam locomotive uncoupled. *National Library of Ireland W. Lawrence collection*

REGULAR ELECTRIC SERVICE COMMENCES 33

Motor-car No.7 at Dunluce Castle; note the gap in the conductor rail for the field entrance.
Ulster Museum, R.J. Welch collection

from the rail and one man who was unable to open his hand at the beginning of the treatment was able to do so after a three weeks course.

Years later, when relating the live rail sitting incident to his daughter, the latter asked, 'And did it really not hurt?' Mr Traill's reply was, 'It hurt like blazes, but we weren't going to let the Inspectors know that.'

The Harbour Tramway Company at Portrush were asked to reduce their toll, which was based on the development of the iron ore trade, as the latter had collapsed, and any ore that was shipped was carried in carts.

A new steam locomotive weighing 10 to 12 tons was to be ordered, and as Messrs. Wilkinson had offered to supply such an engine for £850, to be delivered before 1st March, 1886, their offer was accepted.

Early in 1886 there was some friction between the tramway company and the BNCR re the provision of a uniform for the travelling porter or pilotman employed on the operation of the harbour tramway, the privilege of paying for the clothing of this individual being one which both companies were more than willing to forego.

The original agreement was that each company should provide the travelling porter's uniform on alternate years, and each contribute an agreed proportion of his wage, which was 15s. per week,

Apparently electric working at the beginning of the year was almost non-existent, for the secretary of the BNCR (Mr Cotton) wrote asking if his Company would be right in describing in their advertisements, the

Causeway line as an Electric Tramway. He was informed that electric working was only temporarily suspended pending improvements and a 'great increase' in the electric power. The system would be in full working order for the tourist season, and the line could be duly advertised as an Electric Tramway.

The machinery stock at the end of 1886 was returned as 2 generators, 5 tramcar dynamos, and the rolling stock as 3 steam locomotives, 4 electric cars, 6 trailers, and 14 wagons.

Steam locomotive No. 3 had been named *Dunluce Castle*, and had proved to be very useful in handling the summer traffic.

Work on the Causeway Extension had proceeded throughout the year and Bushmills station was ready for May 1887, as the station master at Bushmills, Henry Chambers, had been given notice that the office in his house would not be required after 1st May.

Steam locomotive No.3 *Dunluce Castle* and trailers at the Giant's Causeway terminus in 1898. Steam locomotive No. 1 or 2 and motor-car No. 9 are on the left. The wire on the white posts in the foreground controlled a catch point. *Author's collection*

Chapter Three

The Extension Opens

The extension came into use on 1st July, 1887, and in many ways it was the pleasantest part of the trip from Portrush to the Causeway. Just about 100 yards short of 'the cross roads where the Electric Car stopped' at Bushmills, the extension left the original line by a passing loop on a sharp curve to the left. The newly-constructed Bushmills station consisted of a substantial stone-finished building, comprising a two-storey dwelling house for the station master, booking office, general waiting room, ladies' waiting room, etc., with a glass canopy along the front of the Waiting Rooms forming a veranda facing the tracks.

The passing loop ended at the Portballintrae Road, the single track crossing the road on the level and at a fairly acute angle. Beyond the road crossing, which was provided with one gate at each side, the line continued on its own right of way like a railway on the level, or on a slight down gradient, and more or less parallel to the road, but about six or eight feet below it, for two or three hundred yards before swinging to the right away from the road and along the edge of the valley of the River Bush. About three-quarters of a mile of straight track brought the line to the River Bush which was crossed by a handsome through-type, three-span, lattice girder bridge, carried 25 ft above river level on two

Victoria Jubilee Bridge, the makers plate standing proud in the centre. *Author*

Clutha Ironwork's makers plate from the Victoria Jubilee Bridge.

Author's collection

massive masonry piers in the river and masonry abutments at either end. The centre span was 70 ft long, the girders being 6 ft deep, whilst the end spans were 22 ft, and 34 ft long respectively, by 5 ft deep, the width between the girders being 12 ft The bridge was built slightly on the skew, the girders on one side being displaced by about 7 ft 6 in. in relation to the girders on the other side. The length between abutments was about 133 ft, and the bridge was built by Messrs. P. & W. Maclellan, Clutha Ironworks, Glasgow.

As 1887 was the year of Queen Victoria's Golden Jubilee, Mr Traill named the bridge 'the Victoria Jubilee Bridge'.

The approaches to the bridge were on embankments, and after crossing the bridge the line passed through the sand hills behind Blackrock Strand for about half a mile before curving to the right, away from the Strand, and climbing at about 1 in 40 to the Causeway Terminus. This, unfortunately, was situated about a mile from the actual entrance to the Causeway, but vested interests in the shape of the hotel proprietors, and the providers of horse-drawn cars probably prevented the line approaching more closely to its target.

The track lay-out at the terminus consisted of a long run-round loop and a fairly long siding. As the tracks were on a falling gradient towards the main line, which itself was on a steep gradient, a catch point was installed, just beyond the station limits. A balance weight of the ball and chain variety kept this point in the de-rail position, but a wire from the point was carried on pulleys and posts like a railway signal wire, back to the terminus so that the pointsman could hold the catch point closed while a tram was making an authorized departure.

A highly ornamental shelter, of corrugated-iron, was provided at the terminus to do duty as booking office, waiting room, etc. This building, which had a pitched roof curving up steeply to a sharp point when viewed on the gable, was brought all the way from Switzerland at a cost of £400.

The siding was used principally by the steam locomotives for fire cleaning, etc.

Generally speaking, the extension was constructed as a railway, with cuttings and embankments to give a reasonably graded line.

The return fares between Portrush and the Causeway were 2s. 3d. first class and 1s. 9d. ordinary, being reduced from 2s. 6d. and 2s. respectively.

A new and larger generator by Ellwell Parker was installed at Walkmills in November 1887 to provide the extra power required to work the anticipated additional traffic due to the extension, 62,004 passengers having been carried in 1887 against 49,117 in 1886, the

Motor-car No. 9 at the Giant's Causeway terminus about 1890.

Author's collection

Steam locomotive No. 1 or 2 and trailers Nos. 13 and 6 at Bushmills about 1889.
Ulster Museum, R.J. Welch collectio

respective figures for goods traffic being 6,188 tons as compared with 5,352 tons.

The electric mileage worked in 1887 was 17,268, steam worked miles being 23,163.

The Company also undertook to carry letters and parcels from Bushmills to Portrush, and vice versa, on behalf of the Postmaster General for a consideration of £100 per annum. Carriage was to be by the 7.10 am, 3.00 pm, and 5.15 pm trains ex-Bushmills, and the 9.00 am, 1.50 pm and 6.05 pm ex-Portrush.

Early in 1888 the board decided to order the following rolling stock: '3 light cars, open, to follow the electric cars and hold about 20 persons, 1 large electric car (open), 2 open cars, full size, and 6 open goods wagons'.

The extension of the tramway opposite the Northern Counties railway station, Portrush, by a length of 75 yards, 'to be macadamized only between the tracks' was authorized in May 1888 as were the construction of additional passing places at the Devil's Punch Bowl and opposite Portballintrae (Gortnee Siding).

At the same time, strangely enough in view of the decision some months earlier to order six new goods wagons, public notice was to be given of the cessation of goods traffic on the harbour tramway, on and

THE EXTENSION OPENS 39

after 1st June, and the BNCR and the harbour tramway were to be notified that on and after 30th June, 1888 the Company would discontinue its use; thus saving the £50 per annum minimum payment to the Harbour Tramway Co., together with the cost of the pilotman's uniform.

Later on in the year, public notice was given that all goods would be unloaded at the Company's Portrush depot. This was done to avoid using the steam locomotives, though presumably at least one engine had to be kept simmering at Portrush to work the electric cars through Causeway Street and Eglinton Street between the depot and the railway station.

The staff was also reduced to five, with a total weekly payroll of £4 4s. 6d., for the winter months, the highest wage being 17s. 6d. and the lowest 10s. Presumably these were based on actual hours worked.

The reduction of staff in the winter months was of course necessary throughout the life of the tramway, due to the seasonal nature of the traffic. This, however, was not so hard on the men as appears at first sight, as the winter was the busy time in the Distillery and the corn and flax mills in Bushmills, so that most of the men found employment in these. Working on the tramway in the summer and in the Distillery and mills in the winter became a tradition for the men throughout the years of operation.

At the Annual General Meeting in February 1883, the engineer reported that five goods wagons had been converted to open passenger cars at a total cost of £200, and the rolling stock return at 31st December, 1888 was given as: 3 steam locos., 4 electric motor cars, 11 passenger trailers, 9 goods wagons; so that the proposal to purchase six passenger cars and six goods wagons apparently only resulted in the conversion just mentioned.

The engineer also stated that the siding at Gortnee had been constructed at a cost of £90, and the extension of the line at Portrush railway station laid at a cost of £75.

Some months later the board decided that the rates per ton for conveying limestone from the Whiterocks to the railway station should be 1s. per ton for lots under 12 tons, and 10d. per ton for lots of 12 tons and over.

The cost of steam working was given as 1s. 4½d. per mile and that of electric working 5½d. per mile, the mileage worked by steam during 1888 being given as 23,588 and by electricity as 12,886.

During 1889 the underground cable between the hydro-electric station at Walkmills and the tramway at Bushmills became so defective that it had to be replaced, and the engineer took the opportunity of avoiding further trouble with underground cables by carrying the new conductor overhead on wooden posts in a similar manner to a telegraph line 'to prevent the deteriorating action experienced upon an underground cable'.

To boost receipts, it was decided to pay a bonus of 1d. in the pound of fares collected to conductors, to encourage the latter to canvas for passengers.

The Company also entered the electricity supply business by agreeing to supply current to the Causeway Hotel at a charge of £10 per annum.

Motor-car No. 4 an the first No. 10 trailer at Giant's Causeway about 1890.
Ulster Museum, R.J. Welch collection

Chapter Four

A Chapter of Accidents

On the early morning of 1st November, 1889 the Portrush lifeboat put out in a raging gale to the assistance of a small schooner which had dragged its anchor in Skerries Roads off the East Strand. The schooner eventually got under way, but the lifeboat was unable to return to Portrush against the force of the gale, so made for Portballintrae.

About 9.30 am, Mr W. A. Traill, who was at the Causeway Hotel, saw the small schooner running before the wind, under shortened sail, in an easterly direction, and then noticed the lifeboat battling with tremendous seas, one of which swept over it, causing it to disappear for some minutes. Mr Traill immediately marshalled some workmen, collected what ropes were available, and hurried with his party to Blackrock Strand, where the lifeboat crew were attempting to beach the boat. With the assistance of Mr Traill and his workers, this operation was successfully completed. Three men, however had been washed overboard by the wave which had engulfed the boat, and were drowned. Their bodies were soon recovered on the Strand, and Mr Traill arranged for a special tram to convey the bodies to the tramshed at Bushmills.

These premises were also used for the inquest, which was held on the following day, so that, so far as is known, this tramway must have been the first, and probably the only, electric tramway, to have had its premises used for an inquest into a lifeboat disaster.

For his assistance in the rescue operations, Mr Traill was awarded the Royal Humane Society's Vellum.

During 1890 the stationary steam engine at Portrush was sold for £100, and the receipts from goods and mineral traffic only accounted for £41 out of total receipts amounting to £2,724.

In 1891 two more goods wagons were converted to passenger trailers.

On 12th September, 1891 the 9.00 pm steam tram from Portrush was scheduled to cross an electric tram from Bushmills at the Giant's Head instead of at Dunluce where they normally crossed. The driver of the steam tram apparently forgot the alteration and the trams met on single track. Quoting from a report of a subsequent board meeting, 'a body threw herself off one of the cars through fright at a collision which seemed to be impending between the steam engine and the electric car coming in the opposite direction, though no collision beyond the slightest contact actually occurred'. The 'body', a Mrs Hall, claimed £2,000 damages, and eventually received £375, the total cost to the Company being £500.

During the summer of 1895 a party of tourists from Preston, Lancashire, were on a boating trip from Portrush when the boat capsized off the Whiterocks. Mr W. A. Traill, who was more than a mile away at the time, hurried to the scene by tram, climbed down the rocky cliffs, and swam out through the breakers. He first reached a young lady, but she refused to be rescued until her mother was saved, so Mr Traill swam on till he came to the husband who was supporting the body of his wife. Mr Traill brought both to land, and then swam out again and brought the daughter ashore, she having remained afloat for over three-quarters of an hour. Only the father and daughter survived.

In acknowledgement of his remarkable feat, quoting, 'the people of Preston presented Mr Traill with a handsome silver bowl, suitably inscribed in commemoration of this extraordinary deed of bravery and endurance.' He acquired also, in due course, a wife, for 30 years afterwards, his second wife having died, the young lady he had saved from drowning in 1895, married him to become the third Mrs Traill.

At 7.30 pm on the evening of 26th August, 1895, Thomas Walne, whilst cycling from Bushmills to Portrush, attempted to turn his bicycle on to the tramway. On striking the kerb the machine was upset, throwing Walne across the track to come to rest with his chest across the live rail. He shouted three times and his fellow cyclist, who had been about 100 yards in the rear, attempted to pull him off the live rail but due to the electric shock, could not do so until he thought of wrapping his mackintosh around his hands. Walne was breathing when removed from the rail and was able to take a drink of brandy, before removal to Bushmills station where he was examined by Dr. David Huey. He had then ceased to breathe though his heart was beating slowly. Artificial respiration was applied but he died about half an hour after the fall.

This accident initiated fundamental changes in the nature of the tramway, for the report submitted by Major Cardew, the Inspector sent by the Board of Trade to investigate the occurrence, condemned the live rail system as it then existed, and made some illuminating comments on the operation of the tramway, as will be seen from the following quotations:

> The line is worked chiefly by steam engines, but electric motors are fitted in a few of the cars.

> The electric power is supplied from a generating station at some distance from the line by means of overhead wires, the energy being obtained from water power.

Board of Trade Regulation	5. Entirely disregarded.
" — "	6. Entirely disregarded
" — "	7 Voltmeter provided not considered satisfactory as due to small size it is difficult for the operator to see whilst operating the turbines.
" — "	9 Entirely disregarded. The additional regulation regarding notice boards is insufficiently attended to. Only three notices observed along the track and these are almost obliterated.
Bye-Law IV.	Disregarded on cars I saw.

I took several tests of the electric pressure at the station at Bushmills, the nearest point on the line to the generating station. The volts in the line varied considerably, the highest reading being 310 volts and the average 290 volts.

Mr Boyd, the Tramway Company's Inspector, stated that the maximum he had observed at the generating station was 360 volts.

In the meantime I think the Company, having regard to the danger shown to exist, should discontinue the use of electrical power until they have carried out the alterations decided upon (i.e., use overhead system, raise the live rail to height of eight feet above ground level, or protect the rail).

Major Cardew's candid criticisms put the Company in a difficult spot, as alterations to the live rail would have involved considerable expenditure.

Pending a decision as to the best permanent solution, the temporary expedient of limiting the voltage was adopted, which in turn meant that only one electric car could be operated. This had the effect of reducing the electrically-worked mileage from 17,323 in 1895 to 6,944 in 1896 and to 4,721 in 1897, the corresponding steam worked mileages being 14,829, 17,279, and 17,797 respectively. .

The cost of steam operation was stated to be about 11d. per mile, and of electric operation 7¾d. per mile in 1896 compared to 1s. 11d. per mile for steam and 4d. per mile for electrical operation in 1889. Though rather unfortunate for the Company, these figures are interesting in showing how the costs of the respective modes of operation decreased with increased mileage and vice versa.

A new steam locomotive was received late in 1895 or early in 1896 from Messrs. Wilkinson, and must have been one of the last they supplied, as a payment of £19 8s. 4d. was made to 'Liquidators of Wilkinson & Co.' in the autumn of 1895. In fact the locomotive may actually have been built by Messrs. Beyer, Peacock & Co., Manchester, a firm which built a number of such engines for Messrs. Wilkinsons, at times when the latter's own works could not cope with all orders on hand.

Permission for the erection of poles and wires in place of the third rail was granted by the Grand Jury in 1896, subject to an Order in Council being obtained. During the following months several firms were approached regarding the terms on which they would undertake the installation of an overhead system of current collection.

The lowest quotations received were £17,000 and £15,000 respectively, and as the Company found it impossible to raise the necessary capital, Mr Traill again acted upon the advice given to prospective tramway and railway proprietors by his brother, the Provost, at the opening ceremony, and decided to do it himself. Carefully observing the proprieties, he resigned his directorship, ordered the necessary materials from the United States of America, and on their arrival, commenced their erection by direct labour. At the Annual General Meeting of the Company in February 1900, in his capacity of engineer, he was able to state in his report that 'On 26th July, 1899 the Company changed from side-rail to overhead conductor without a day's interruption of traffic.'

Previously, at their meeting on 27th November, 1899, the board authorized the allotment of £5,000 in Debentures and £3,000 in Preference Shares to Mr Traill in payment for his contract for the installation of the overhead system and stated 'As Mr Traill has completed his contract and been paid, the Board now co-opt him as a Director.'

And so the end of the 19th century may be taken as the end of the pioneering period of the Giant's Causeway Electric Tramway with its unique system of current collection and of traction equipment. Henceforth it was fundamentally the same as the electric systems then being adopted in all progressive cities throughout the world; but with a rugged individualist like Mr W. A. Traill at the helm, and its finances continuously in a state of balance so delicate that a wet week in July, or a heat wave at August Bank Holiday week-end, could swing the annual receipts to loss or profit respectively, the line could not but display many idiosyncrasies, some delightful and some not, but most of them interesting.

Chapter Five

The 'Trolley' Takes Over

Once the overhead system had been installed it might have been expected that the Company's troubles would have been over for a time at least, but such was not the case. The closing months of 1899 and the beginning of 1900, saw the Company engaged in a lawsuit with the Portrush Urban District Council in which the latter sought to force the Company to abandon electric working through the streets of Portrush. This suit apparently dragged on for most of a year, because it was only in October 1900 that it was recorded that the Council had now agreed to the use of the overhead system on condition that:

> the pole at the Methodist Church Bend be kept lighted from sunset till sunrise on every day of the year, and that the pole on Springhill is rendered safe.

Meanwhile, as Board of Trade Regulations permitted operation at 500 to 550 volts with the overhead system of current collection, in July of 1900 an order for a new dynamo was placed with the Electric Construction Company at a cost of £265. At the same time an order for a new turbine at £150 was placed with Messrs. Turnbulls.

Motor-car No. 23 at 'the curve' in Portrush with a good view of the overhead equipment.
Oakwood collection

In 1897 two new trailers had been added 'bringing the total number of cars up to 19, open and covered' and 'one of the tramway engines required considerable repair, which may not become necessary' (presumably if the overhead system was installed) and the rolling stock at the end of 1897 was given as 4 steam locos., 4 electric cars, 15 trailers and 7 wagons.

Two new electric cars of toast-rack type, Nos. 20 and 21, were added in 1899 for the inauguration of the overhead system, and the rolling stock at the beginning of 1900 was given as 3 steam locos. (one removed from stock in 1898), 4 electric cars, 17 trailers, which indicates that two of the old motor-cars continued in use, though presumably with new motors to suit the higher voltage.

There were several interesting occurrences in 1901. Permission was obtained from a Mr Douglas for a flag-man to use Gallery Hill, between Dunluce and Portballintrae Road. At this point the road and tramway rounded the end of a promontory by means of a sharp curve, only a low stone wall being between the tramway and the almost sheer drop of over 150 ft to the rocks at the sea's edge. The writer well remembers the flag-man's hut, similar to the sentry-box still used by night-watchmen,

No. 21 heads towards the causeway full of tourists for the Giant's Causeway.
Oakwood collection

perched on a narrow ledge which existed at one point between the aforementioned wall and the precipitous drop to the rocks below. From this vantage point the flag-man could see the line from the passing loop at Dunluce to a point about 100 yards from the Portrush end of the passing loop at Portballintrae Road. When a Portrush-bound tram reached this point, it frequently had to reverse to the loop, as the flag-man had given the road to a tram from the Portrush direction.

As this was one of the most awkward bends on the line and permission was only then being sought to establish a flag-man at it, it would appear that the signalling system generally was only commenced at this time, though telephones between Bushmills and the Causeway terminus, and between Bushmills and the hydro-electric power station at Walkmills, permitted a fairly reasonable system of tram control to be maintained. The higher speeds of the new cars, however, would have increased the possibility and danger of a head-on collision at blind corners, especially as the new cars could each pull two trailers and continuous brakes were not fitted.

Another point which had caused the Company some irritation and inconvenience was a (presumably) recent edict of the Board of Trade that the steam locomotives should pull only two trailers. A letter protesting against this limitation was sent to the Board of Trade and must have achieved relaxation of this regulation, because trains of up to four cars were operated by the steam locomotives until the latter were taken out of service some decades later. If more than two trailers were used, however, two conductors (or a conductor and brakesman) had to be carried in addition to the driver, so that the hand-brake on at least two trailers would be available in case of emergency.

Towards the end of the year, the board ordered that a third electric car 'the same as those already there', be ordered for delivery by 1st March, 1902. This car was duly put into service in 1902 and cost £450.

A piece of good news for the tramway, and of interest to railway enthusiasts generally as showing commendable enterprise on the part of the Belfast & Northern Counties Railway, was recorded in the board's minutes as follows:

> It is understood that Messrs. Holden of Larne have arranged with the Northern Counties Railway Co. to build for their use a Special Train of Saloon Carriages and that they propose sending down from 300 to 400 tourists daily for at least 3 months every summer.

This train was actually built and consisted of three saloon bogie coaches, bogie dining saloon, and six-wheeled van, and was known to the railway staff as 'the Holden Train'. An interesting sidelight on the Holden tours was the fact that each tourist was presented with a token or medallion bearing a portrait of Mr Holden in person.

The year 1903 opened with the board of directors offering to sell the tramway to the Midland Railway Co., which had just purchased the Belfast & Northern Counties Railway and formed the Northern Counties Committee (NCC). The Midland Railway, however, declined to purchase. By coincidence the Midland happened to be one of the few railway companies in Great Britain to own and operate an electric tramway for many years - between Ashby-de-la-Zouch and Burton-on-Trent.

Another new turbine was ordered by Mr Traill in the spring of 1903 'not to be installed during the fishing season without the written permission of Sir Francis Macnaghten'.

A melancholy occurrence was the accidental killing of two children by one of the locomotives in June of 1903.

Two less serious mishaps occurred during that summer. A Mrs Jackson's best coat was damaged due to part of the paint on one of the cars showing greater affinity for the coat than the car. When Mr Jackson claimed £3 damages, the board directed that he be informed that the 'Company could not afford to pay for grand clothes if people chose to tour in them', together with the advice that benzine was an excellent medium for removing paint stains! In due course Mr Jackson accepted £1 as reasonable compensation.

One Matthew Craig received even more cavalier treatment. On lodging a claim for damage to his trousers caused by a piece of hot coke from the engine burning a hole in them, he was informed that this was one of the ordinary hazards of travelling and that no claim could be entertained. However, he eventually received 10s. compensation.

It would appear from the above that the Company expected any person who wished to travel on their services to take somewhat unusual precautions in the matter of attire.

Transport of iron ore was again in the picture in 1904, when a Mr Stopford wrote to the Company regarding the carriage of that commodity from the Dunluce Mines to Portrush. He was informed with more bluntness than politeness that the 'Tramway Company cannot deposit the ore in the streets of Portrush nor have they any connection with the Harbour'. However if the Iron Ore Company cared to make a siding from their mine to the tramway and from the tramway to a siding in Portrush, the tramway company would carry the ore. Apparently this handsome offer was not accepted, as there is no record of any construction being carried out.

Bushmills station with trailer No. 10 at the rear of a short train. The tracks leading to the right served the car sheds, originally they continued to Main Street in Bushmills but this extension was lifted in the 1890s. *Oakwood collection*

Purchase of a new steam locomotive and four additional cars was proposed in the following year (1905), but the engineer reported that 'no engines for tramways are now made', and this also disposed of the four cars as the necessary motive power would not then have been available, the existing 17 trailers being as much as the three locomotives and three electric cars could handle.

Later in the year the Company noted with alarm that the NCC had placed motor charabancs on the road to the Giant's Causeway and to Carrick-a-Rede, in opposition to the tramway. When approached by the Tramway Co., the Northern Counties Committee stated that the motors were only for the amusement of the people staying at the Northern Counties Hotel, 'but a few days afterwards the town was plastered with placards stating that the buses were running to the Causeway'.

The end of 1906 and beginning of 1907 saw the extension of the telephone system from Bushmills to Portrush, the wires being carried on insulators fixed to the poles supporting the tramway overhead system. This meant that the two termini, Bushmills station and Walkmills Power Station, were now all on the telephone and this permitted a measure of 'Centralized Tram Control'.

The year 1907 also saw the installation of a more powerful electric generator in Walkmills Power Station, the generator having been purchased from the Electric Construction Company (ECC) for £350.

A new enclosed electric car had been ordered from America for delivery in 1907. Unfortunately some hitch occurred, as in January 1908 was recorded the following:

> Much disappointment has been caused by the non-arrival from America of the body for a new electrical car after the electrical machinery had been provided.

Apparently, however, Mr Traill adopted his usual 'do it yourself?' tactics and built a body locally during 1907, as he stated that a new electric car would be ready for the coming (1908) season, and the rolling stock return for 31st December, 1908 gave the number of electric cars as 4, against 3 for 31st December, 1907. The expenditure on the car was given as £363 15s. 5d. for the 'machinery' and £107 1s. 4d. for woodwork.

It must have been a success, for a tender from the Malleable Steel Casting Co. of Pendleton, for the supply of an electric car truck at a cost of £30, was accepted in August 1908, and in January 1909 the engineer stated that he proposed to have another electric car ready for the coming season.

The rolling stock return at 31st December, 1909 was given as: 2 steam locomotives, 5 electric cars, 18 trailers, 1 wagon, and this suggests that possibly a trailer had been used as the source of the body for the new car. This matter is discussed more fully in the section on rolling stock.

A new car-shed at Bushmills was erected in 1909 at a cost of £84 6s. This presumably was really the addition of a second bay to the existing single road shed.

The rapid urban expansion in Great Britain in the early years of the century created an unprecedented demand for stone for road making, and the output from Craignahuilliagh Quarry, operated by the Giant's Causeway Columnar Basalt Co., found a ready market. As the quarry was situated about a mile from Portrush, all stone for export either by sea or by rail had to be transported to the harbour or railway station by horse-drawn carts. This restricted output and increased costs to such an extent, that serious consideration was given to alternative methods of transport between quarry and ship, and in 1910 Mr Traill submitted to the Privy Council, plans for extensions to the tramway to permit carriage of stone from the quarry over the tramway to the harbour and railway station, and at the same time improve the working of passenger traffic by relieving the congestion in Eglinton Street outside the railway station.

One scheme proposed by Mr Traill was the construction of a completely new 3 ft gauge line on the landward side of the coast road, from the quarry to a point opposite the Gas Works, where the new line

THE 'TROLLEY' TAKES OVER 51

Robert Scott at the controls of motor-car No. 23 at Giant's Causeway. *Oakwood collection*

Waiting for passengers at Portrush station. *Oakwood collection*

would have left the road in a westerly direction and curved round to pass down Dunluce Street, across Eglinton Street in front of the railway station and join the harbour branch of the railway, along which an additional rail was to be laid, just as it had been originally in 1883. This would have permitted the construction of a passenger loading point between the crossing of Eglinton Street and the junction with the harbour branch.

An alternative scheme submitted by Mr Traill involved the construction of a branch siding from the existing tramway to the quarry, and the laying of a new line along Crock-na-Mac Road, across the Coleraine Road, past the rear of the Metropole Hotel, through the railway embankment by means of a tunnel, and then along the sea-side of the station, to join the harbour branch.

Either of the above schemes would have obviated the necessity for the tramcars to pass along Eglinton Street and Causeway Street, both of which were very congested with vehicles and pedestrians at holiday times.

A tram in Causeway Street Portrush making its way towards Bushmills.

Oakwood collection

Although the Board of Works gave its approval to at least one of the above proposals, unfortunately both the Antrim County Council and Portrush Urban District Council refused to sanction the construction, and nothing further was done.

In passing, although not concerning the tramway, it may be mentioned, that one proposal for facilitating the shipment of stone from a quarry was the construction of a telpher line, or overhead cable-way, from the quarry across the coast road and sandhills to a point off the East Strand at which it was proposed to construct a loading berth for ships.

Another matter which was causing the Company some anxiety about this time (1911) was the probable disastrous effect on the working of the tramway, should an extended period of drought occur so as to cause a water shortage during the peak holiday season. Few transport undertakings can have been so bedevilled by the weather as the Giant's Causeway Tramway. If the weather was wet, the number of passengers was reduced, and if the weather was exceptionally good (a much rarer occurrence), power to cope with the resulting rush of traffic might not be available.

As if the above tribulations were not enough, the fact that the River Bush was (and is) a salmon river of note, meant that in times of drought water had to be allowed to run to waste over the Salmon Leap without doing any work in the turbines. It can be appreciated that this led to a certain amount of friction between the local landowner and the tramway company. Both sides were strong believers in the adage that 'possession is nine points of the law', and as far as can be gathered from the reports of the proceedings, if either protagonist felt that an adjustment of the sluice gates would improve his interests, he ordered the appropriate adjustment to be made without troubling to consult the other party to the agreement, and one gets the impression that during periods of low water, the sluice gates must have been going up and down like the horses on a merry-go-round.

In view of the above, together with the fact that the original agreement on water rights was for a period of 35 years, of which 28 years had passed, it was decided that an alternative source of power should be provided. An order was placed with Messrs. Fielding & Platt for the supply of an electricity generating plant, powered by a gas engine and suction gas plant, at a cost of £470, and this was installed at Portrush depot during 1911 at a total cost of over £500.

The weather during the summer of 1913 was unusually good, and the gas engine plant was then brought into use for the first time, due to shortage of water.

A steam-hauled tram making its way along Eglinton Street, Portrush. *Oakwood Collection*

Portrush station where the tram vies with horse-drawn transport for visitors.
Oakwood collection

Chapter Six

The First World War

The outbreak of war in August 1914 hit the tramway badly as the holiday season came to a premature end, with consequent adverse effect on receipts. However, energetic representations by the management to the appropriate authority at Westminster resulted in the tramway being taken over by the Government just as the railways were, and any losses on working were made good by the Government.

The year 1915 saw the passing of several persons connected with the tramway. In February occurred the death of Dr. Antony Traill, chairman of the Company from its formation, whilst Mr David Fall, manager and secretary since 1883, died on 5th May. Another employee committed suicide during the summer.

A peculiar case of malicious damage also occurred in the summer of 1915, when a tramcar was thrown off the rails.

On 6th May, 1916 the tramway joined what must have been the very exclusive circle of British tramway systems to have suffered damage from a naval engagement.

At about 11.00 am on that day, the coaster *Wheatear* on her way from Coleraine to Great Britain, was confronted off Runkerry Head, near the Giant's Causeway, by a German submarine on the surface. The *Wheatear* was armed with a 4in. gun and shots were exchanged. *Wheatear* turned back to Blackrock Bay, off Portballintrae, and the submarine, about four miles off-shore, maintained a continuous hail of 6 in. shells, one of which formed a crater about 10 ft diameter and 5 ft deep, only 120 yards from a house on the outskirts of the village.

Two tramway men off duty, and who happened to be at Gortnee siding, had their clothes torn by splinters. Another splinter severed the straining wire of one of the poles supporting the overhead wire. This was the only damage resulting from a bombardment which lasted about 2 hours. Mr Traill, who watched the engagement, reckoned that about 250 shots were exchanged.

Many tramway men had joined the Forces, and by July 1916, six had been killed and two wounded, a high proportion out of what cannot have been much more than 20 or 25 employees. The body of one man, Samuel Spiers, was given a military funeral and was taken from Portrush station to Bushmills by special tramcar draped with Union Jack, crepe, and wreaths.

As the two surviving steam locomotives had been practically idle from the outbreak of war, the Company optimistically enquired of the

Ministry of Munitions if the latter would like to purchase them, but the Ministry stated that they had no 3 ft gauge railway on which to use them.

Apparently more success was achieved in 1917 in disposing of the gas engine plant as the Cork, Bandon & South Coast Railway received £18 3s. 3d. as half the carriage on the plant to some purchaser.

On 16th December, 1917 a blizzard occurred, which brought down many of the wooden poles on the power line from Walkmills to Bushmills, and also four steel poles at Gortnee.

Tramcar services were perforce temporarily suspended, and jaunting cars were used, but even these were not immune from mishap, because the shafts of one car broke, and 'two passengers were more or less injured'.

The wooden poles and power line between Walkmills and Bushmills had been repaired by 3rd January, 1918 but the tram service had not been resumed by the end of the month.

The number of passengers in 1917 was 48,000, compared with 72,000 in 1916 and 155,000 in 1913, receipts in 1916 being only £2,376 compared with £4,635 in 1913. The Company accordingly received £2,289 compensation from the Government Irish Railway Executive Committee.

Disputes about the water rights at Walkmills, which had extended over a number of years came to a head in 1918, when the original lease for a period of 35 years from 1883 expired, culminating in a law suit. Pending the result of the latter, consideration was given to purchasing power from Portrush Urban District Council which was contemplating the provision of an electricity distribution system in the town. Mr Traill pointed out to the Council the advantages to the latter of having the tramway as a customer. In summer, when the lighting load would be low, the tramway load would be high, whilst in winter, when the lighting load would be high, the tramway load would be small, and so the power station plant would be kept gainfully employed throughout the year. One of the main stumbling blocks in the negotiations with the Council was that of estimating the current consumption of the cars, no metering apparatus apparently being available.

However, the law suit was settled more or less amicably early in 1920, before negotiations with the Urban District Council had crystallized.

Chapter Seven

Motor Charabanc and Omnibus Competition

Being under Government control during the war, the tramway had been able to obtain materials for necessary repairs but non-essentials such as painting had had to be kept to a minimum, so during 1920 a determined effort was made to reduce the back-log of such work. Many of the cars and the two steam locomotives were repainted, and the Company indulged contemporary fashion to the extent of using ferro-concrete posts in fencing around the depot and by putting a large number of ferro-concrete sleepers in the track.

Early in 1921, the Company received £8,437 as its share of the Government compensation to the Irish Railways Companies.

Until 1921 no means of measuring the power output of the generating stations or the power consumed by the cars had been available, but in that year a tramcar meter was purchased from Messrs. Chamberlain & Hookham for £7 19s.

It was also decided that, as Government control and Government compensation had ceased, the eight hour day and payment for overtime would also have to cease, while drastic reductions in wages and the number of employees would have to be made. These decisions were accompanied by the sentiment:

> It is hoped that the employees have been able to lay by something during the time high wages were being paid.

By 1922, the motor-bus and charabanc era had got into its stride, and competition on the Portrush–Portstewart route had become so intense that operators found it unprofitable. They then turned their attention to the Portrush–Giant's Causeway–Carrick-a-Rede route, providing a half-hourly service to the Causeway at the tram fare (2s. return). The return fare between Portrush and Carrick-a-Rede was 4s.

The tramway company countered by reducing the return fare between Portrush and the Causeway to 1s. and, in conjunction with Messrs. Weir Bros., charabanc owners, Bushmills, provided a combined tram and charabanc service from Portrush to Carrick-a-Rede at 2s. 6d. return. The results of this spirited counter-attack were most gratifying as the competition collapsed. The tramway conveyed over 3,000 passengers to the Causeway at 1s. return on August Bank Holiday, and up to 60 passengers a day to Carrick-a-Rede at 2s. 6d. return, of which the tramway received 1s. and Weir Bros. 1s. 6d.

Another incident suggests that the rivalry almost blossomed into a physical war, as 'the large charabanc, *The Knut*, collided with a tramcar in Causeway Street, causing considerable damage, but no personal injury'.

It was decided that one car; No. 9, would be sufficient to maintain the winter service, Robert Scott being detailed to carry on single-handed as motor-man and conductor. The permanent-way gang was paid-off on 11th November, and the total wages bill for the remaining staff of eight was just over £17 per week.

A letter enquiring if the NCC (now part of the London Midland & Scottish Railway after the 1923 grouping), would consider purchasing or absorbing the tramway was sent to Mr Pepper, the manager of the Northern Counties Committee, but the Railway Company politely refused to purchase.

In spite of the not entirely satisfactory financial results, extensive maintenance works were continued throughout 1922 and 1923, the tramway being closed for two weeks in April 1923 to permit the track being raised by from 9 to 11 in. at Clooney Hill and the 'S' curve; This was necessitated by the County Surveyor having the roadway resurfaced.

Car No. 9 as originally converted in 1909 to operate from the overhead system. Note the first class compartment, as well as the bell and trolley hook at each end of the roof. Former motor-car No. 7 is in tow. *Author's collection*

Whilst the NCC authorities may have had no desire to acquire the tramway, they were quite prepared to be neighbourly, and in 1923 carried out boiler repairs to steam locomotive No. 3, *Dunluce Castle*, at a cost of £12 10s. 4d.

Two complete sets of tramcar wheels were also ordered, one set for a motor-car and one set for a trailer. The order had been placed with the British Griffin Chilled Iron & Steel Co., Barrow, and work had begun on the four pairs of wheels sent to them when the firm went into liquidation. This put the tramway company in rather a spot, as the wheels were of chilled cast-iron as commonly used in America, but which were not so commonly used in the British Isles, and Mr Traill experienced considerable trouble, before the wheels were eventually sent to the English Electric Co.'s Dick Kerr Works in Preston. This firm proposed to fit the normal British type of wheel with cast-iron centre and steel tyre. The report of the engineer, Mr Traill, on the matter contained several interesting pieces of information, viz.:

> The cost of the steel-tyred wheels might be three or four times the cost of the chilled cast-iron wheels, but the treads of the steel wheels could be turned up several times, whereas the chilled wheels were useless when the treads got chipped or worn into flats. Some chilled wheels might last for five years, others give up after two or three months.

The return fare between Portrush and Giant's Causeway, reduced to 1s. in 1922, was raised to 2s. in 1923, and the receipts for Easter Monday and Tuesday in 1923 at £110 15s. 2d., were the highest since the tramway started, the previous highest having been £44 16s. 4d.

An important step taken in 1923 was the abolition of first-class cars. Prior to this the saloon cars and certain of the open cars had been reserved for first-class passengers at a higher fare.

Another innovation was the employment of a ticket inspector at a wage of 35s. per week.

The receipts on 13th July, always a big day in that area, when the farming community within a radius of 20 miles converged on 'the Port' (as Portrush is known locally), amounted to £122, or £22 more than the previous highest, and the receipts for July and August 1923 exceeded the total receipts for 1922.

This satisfactory state of affairs was considered to be due to having smashed the charabanc traffic in the previous year, and to the efforts of the manager of the Northern Counties Committee in pushing Portrush as a holiday resort by instituting a 4s. day return ticket from Belfast to Portrush every day. Some of the success was attributed to the fact that on 'big days' the tramway company put out a blackboard advertising a half-hour service each way 'and maintained the service as well'. 'Another point that helped was that no fare was mentioned on the blackboard, and the Belfast people paid no attention to the fares charged until they boarded the cars, and of course when they came back they were satisfied with the day's outing.' The Company could apply psychology when it was so minded.

The possibility of supplying electricity to Bushmills for lighting purposes was also investigated in 1923, and even caused some heated exchanges between members of the board, and a demand in the following year for the resignation of Mr Traill. As the latter was the largest shareholder and debenture holder he was in a fairly strong position, but resigned from the position of manager, in favour of Mr McCurdy who became manager and secretary Mr Traill remaining as Engineer and Chairman.

The Northern Counties Committee carried out further repairs costing £25 16s. 11d., to the steam locomotive *Dunluce Castle* in 1924, and also supplied 300 second-hand sleepers at 2s. 6d. each. Each railway sleeper could be sawn into two narrow gauge sleepers as used on the tramway.

The water in the Bush River was adequate to keep the five electric cars working 'nearly every day' throughout the summer of 1924, but the engineer, Mr Traill, felt that an alternative source of power should be available. Consequently, work had been commenced on building a new power station at Portrush depot, and by the end of the year, Mr Traill had placed a firm order with the National Gas Engine Co., for a 132 h.p. crude oil engine, at a price of £1,200. This engine was to be of the horizontal, twin cylinder type, and was to be delivered before 1st May, 1925. The Electric Construction Company generator installed at Walkmills in 1907 having given such satisfactory service, an order for a modern version of that generator, to cost £324 19s. 1d., was placed with the ECC.

Meanwhile, in February 1925 a horizontal shaft on the hydroelectric plant broke, and it was decided to suspend the tramway service from 9th March until further notice to permit extensive repairs to be carried out to the plant at Walkmills. 'It may cost a good deal of money but we can't avoid it.' The repairs consisted principally of replacing the wooden teeth in the several gear wheels at a cost of over £100 (about £90 for timber and £25 for shaping the teeth), and providing a new shaft to replace the broken one. The cost of the latter and some other repairs came to £59 9s. 8d.

The new power station at Portrush was opened by Mrs W. A. Traill on 1st July, 1925 with considerable ceremony and a write-up in the local press, in which the power station was described as being 'a handsome

MOTOR CHARABANC AND OMNIBUS COMPETITION

A tram leaving from Portrush station for Bushmills, past the town's impressive town hall, and the buses and cars competing for visitor traffic. *Oakwood collection*

building in hammered black basalt, the corners, etc., being relieved by white moulded brick quoins.' Attention was drawn to the fact that it was also the centenary of the opening of the Stockton & Darlington Railway.

Later on in the month the chairman and engineer, Mr Traill, reported to the board as follows:

> The auxiliary generating station at Portrush Depot has been completed and was opened for the supply of current on 1st July, as was promised to Mr McCurdy (the manager), since when he has been able to give a half-hour service daily from 7.20 am to 10.30 pm The twin engine has given entire satisfaction, working with the greatest smoothness and being governed within very close limits, doing the traffic from the railway station to the Ballymoney Road siding, and later to the Dunluce Siding, beyond which the traffic is worked from Walkmills.
>
> With the very dry month of June and first half of July, the water in the Bush River fell very low, and the half-hourly services could not have been maintained from Walkmills alone, in fact it takes all its work to keep up the services on the half-section of the line.
>
> The new generator (at Portrush) has not yet been able to give out its full power of 550 volts, but we hope it will be able to do so with more experience of its working.

Tram No. 22 with Dan Jamieson at the controls and William Glass as the conductor.
Oakwood collection

Nos 7 and 20 at the Giant's Causeway terminus. *Oakwood collection*

During June, a party of 400 Americans had been successfully conveyed to the Giant's Causeway and back, the largest single party ever carried at one time since the opening of the tramway. Seven trains of cars starting at intervals of two minutes took the whole party. As there were only five motor-cars, the two steam locomotives must have been in use also.

An increase in receipts amounting to £201 for the first 22 days in July 1925 over those for the corresponding period in July 1924 was attributed to the availability of the new power station.

Two items of expenditure occurring as such in the accounts for the last time towards the end of 1925 were: '3 loads of bog-wood for Engines £3 15s.' and 'coke for engines £22 6s. 1d.'

Item No. 1 may be rather unintelligible to a townsman or to a 'Sassenach', but refers to wood obtained from the trunks of fir trees which had been buried for hundreds of years in peat bogs. This wood is very resinous, a splinter burning like a candle if ignited, and the '3 loads of bog-wood' were used as fire lighters in the steam locomotives.

As a matter of interest, a total of £93 19s. 7d. was spent in 1925 on coke for the engines.

Although fuel for the engines does not again appear as such in the Company's accounts, the writer has definitely seen one of the engines working a train in the latter half of 1926, if not later, and it is probable that they were pressed into service occasionally even later than that, though in October 1925 the engineer had advised:

> that we should absolutely discontinue the using of the two steam tramway engines, and sell them for scrap if a higher price cannot be obtained for them. They are very expensive in fuel, upkeep, drivers, and cleaners' wages, etc., and heavy on the permanent way and were only found useful to accommodate large excursion parties, Laharna Hotel parties, NCC and Henry McNeill parties, etc., and the receipts from the passengers so carried did not meet expenses.

The same report stated that the new power house and plant cost £2,500, and also that if services were maintained throughout the winter, a deficit of £838 would have accumulated by 31st May, 1926. There was no alternative to closing down for the winter, only three employees being retained, one at Portrush, one at Walkmills, and one as motor-man to run a car once a month as there was a clause in the Company's Act of Parliament which permitted the County to foreclose and take possession if the tramway was shut for a month. The manager and the engineer were prepared to take reduced salaries.

An approach was again made to the NCC to take over the tramway, but the Railway Company again declined, and in view of this, Robt. Maxwell was detailed to look after Walkmills, W. Sinclair to look after the oil-engine at the new power station, and Robert Scott to be both motor-man and conductor on the monthly tram, all at reduced wages from 31st October.

It was even suggested that no attempt should be made to carry passengers during the following summer of 1926.

This depressing proposal contrasts strangely with the optimism which prompted the construction of the new power station a few months earlier and is hard to understand, unless it was part of a wily scheme to counter in advance, awkward demands, such as increases in wages, local rates, or other undesirable expenditure, on the Company's rather meagre financial resources.

The Causeway terminus looking back towards Bushmills and Portrush.
Author's collection

Chapter Eight

Difficult Years

From the tone of the report of October 1925 it might reasonably have been assumed that things had come to such a pass, that only lack of the funds necessary to defray funeral expenses prevented the demise of the tramway.

However, by June 1926 it could be reported that the service had been resumed at Easter, and that, as might have been expected by anyone familiar with the Giant's Causeway Tramway Co., the three employees retained throughout the winter did not just sit hibernating in their respective power stations or monthly tramcar, but had devoted their time to overhauling the cars and renewing the emergency wires on the electric poles (stirrup wires at crossarms) 'which had been badly rusted after so many years put up'.

The General Strike had dislocated the Whitsun traffic and the May receipts were disappointing, though on 27th May a party of 1,000 from the Co-operative Union Conference in Belfast had been accommodated to the Giant's Causeway. The Railway Company and the charabanc owners were not able to provide accommodation so the tramway company undertook the job. As all the party wanted to travel at the same time, Mr McCurdy, the manager, hired the number of charabanc necessary to augment the five trams of electric cars. 'It poured rain all day.' The hire of the charabanc cost £26 8s., spread over four operators.

In August 1926, Mr McCurdy, the manager, had to retire due to ill health, and in September Mr Michael Keenan, station master on the NCC at Ballymena and formerly station master at Portrush, was appointed manager and secretary.

Mr William Chambers, also an employee of the NCC, was appointed assistant engineer.

Again it was decided to suspend services from the end of October, partly to permit a thorough overhaul of the overhead system and partly because

> the winter receipts are not worth making provision for, and no hardship is experienced by the public who by preference patronise the Bushmills and Coleraine motor buses.

Gross Receipts for 1926 were £3,567 15s. 2½d. and Expenditure was £2,839 16s. 8½d. After making provision for interest on Debentures and Mortgage Accounts, there was a nett deficit of £809 8s. 6d.

Over the years, repeated repairs to the carriageway of the coast road by means of successive layers of tar-macadam had raised the surface of the roadway above the tram track in many places, and water from the road ran on to the track, causing maintenance difficulties. The tramway company, therefore, at the end of the summer of 1927 approached the Ministry of Labour for a grant towards the cost of employing men to raise the tramway above the roadway again. As the Ministry refused to contribute towards this cost, the proposed raising of the track was abandoned for the time being.

Tramway services were suspended from the end of October 1927 until 1st May, 1928, except for a few days at Christmas and a week at Easter.

The financial results for 1927 were rather better, the Gross Receipts rising to £4,213 10s. 5d., Expenditure being £2,931 3s. 4d. The Company made 400 ferro-concrete sleepers during the winter and placed them in stock, and the generator driving belt at Walkmills, which had been in use since 1918, was replaced at a cost of £47 6s. 5d.

Due to motor bus competition, the Portrush–Dunluce single fare was reduced from 8d. to 6d. and the Portrush–Whiterocks and Giant's Causeway–Bushmills single fares were reduced from 6d. to 3d. Special Excursion Tickets from Bushmills to Portrush were introduced at 6d. single and 1s. return.

Tramway services were again suspended from 31st October, 1928 until 1st May, 1929, except for a few days at Christmas and at Easter.

During the 1927-1928 winter, work on raising the track was commenced. The County Surveyor decided to scarify the roadway before re-macadamizing it, and the tramway company thriftily cashed in on this by using the material removed during the scarifying process as the ballast necessary to raise the track to the required level, a lift varying from 6 in. to 14 in. at different places.

About £90 was expended on second-hand sleepers at 3s. each from the Great Northern Railway and NCC, and £35 on second-hand rails at £3 per ton from the latter company. Two miles of the Portrush–Bushmills section and a mile of the Bushmills–Causeway section were re-sleepered and re-ballasted in this operation.

The NCC also supplied some trolley-heads at a total cost of £4 14s. 10d. Presumably these were cast in York Road shops, from a sample head. An interesting point about the second-hand rails obtained from that Company was that they came from the Ballycastle Railway. When the Northern Counties Committee took over the Ballycastle Railway, the rails which were of light section, were badly worn and the NCC relaid the line with heavier section second-hand rails from the broad-gauge line.

Up to 1930, only two cars, Numbers 9 and 23, had been provided with head lamps, and these of a somewhat primitive kind consisting of an approximately 3 in. diameter hole in the dashboards, a bull's-eye glass being fitted in the hole, with a lamp box behind. In 1930, however, proper tramcar headlights were purchased from Siemens' at a cost of £4 5s. 7d., and these were fitted in due course to cars Numbers 20 and 21.

On 28th August, 1930 one of the conductors slipped when passing from one car to another, and received such injuries to his ankle from the wheels of the following car, that his leg had to be amputated above the ankle. He subsequently resumed work in Walkmills power station.

A second accident, this time to a 'flag-boy' also occurred. He was found below the running-board of a tram, and though not apparently seriously injured, died the following morning.

On 16th April, 1931 the two remaining steam locomotives, Numbers 3 and 4, were sold for £25 to a Mr Faris who at that time had a contract for supplying stone from his quarry on the bank of the nearby River Bann for the construction of a breakwater at the mouth of that river. For this purpose he had constructed a narrow-gauge railway about 1½ miles long and the two locomotives were used to operate the trains on this line.

At the September meeting of the board, the chairman's speech was delightfully paradoxical. Commencing on an optimistic note, with characteristic grandiloquence he proposed 'that 1933 should be made a Jubilee Commemoration Year of the introduction of electricity as a motive power for traction purposes', and modestly suggested that the Governor of Northern Ireland (The Duke of Abercorn), the Prime Minister of Northern Ireland (Lord Craigavon), the Governor-General of the then Irish Free State, and the Lord Mayor of Belfast, be asked to give their patronage to the celebrations. The NCC would be asked to co-operate in organising at Portrush a meeting of eminent scientific men of the day, at which examples of electrical apparatus and equipment would be displayed. A prominent item in the proceedings was to be the entertainment of the distinguished guests to luncheon in the Causeway Hotel, transport between Portrush and the hotel presumably to be by tastefully decorated electric tram.

From these dizzy and delectable heights of splendours to come, Mr Traill then descended somewhat abruptly to the rather less palatable realm of fact by stating that the receipts for the year under review (1931) were down due to bad weather and to competition from buses and motors which had necessitated the return fare to the Causeway being reduced to 1s. 'Others were charging 1s. 6d.'

As a consequence of this unsatisfactory financial result, the chairman, manager, and assistant engineer had agreed voluntarily to a 20 per cent reduction in their salaries from 1st November until sometime next spring, the reduction to be a debt on the Company. Only three men at 30s. per week each were to be retained throughout the winter, the older men, Robert Maxwell and Robert Scott, were to go on unemployment benefit 'much as we regret it'.

The year 1932 was a rather depressing year, as another conductor slipped when passing from car to car and had to have his leg amputated below the knee, while some anxiety arose about Mr Traill's health, and he was not able to be present at the December meeting of the board.

Early in 1933 Mr Traill asked that, due to his state of health, the Jubilee Celebrations be cancelled. He passed away on 6th July, 1933 at the age of 89.

In accordance with a previous agreement, Mrs Traill succeeded her husband as chairman of the Company, and Mr Chambers was promoted to chief engineer. Mr Keenan, who had previously intimated his desire to retire from the post of manager and secretary became managing director and secretary.

At the beginning of 1934, revised fares were introduced as follows:

	Single	Return
Portrush–Giant's Causeway	1s.	1s. 6d.
Portrush–Bushmills	9d.	1s. 2d.
Portrush–Dunluce	6d.	9d.
Portrush–Whiterocks (Ballybogey Road)	3d.	—
Bushmills–Giant's Causeway		

By September it could be stated that the reduced fares had resulted in an increase of £254 in receipts and of 16,696 in the number of passengers carried up till the end of August. The Northern Counties Committee had also co-operated by advertising the tramway's excursions with its own, at no charge to the tramway company.

Chapter Nine

Break downs and Bargains

During August 1935 motor-car Number 9 misbehaved itself badly. Having burnt out one armature, which was then replaced, Number 9 proceeded to burn out the replacement, and had to finish the month's working running on one motor and pulling only one trailer instead of the usual two.

Work carried out during the end of 1935 and the beginning of 1936 included the installation of electric light in Portrush depot with cabling obtained at scrap price, and the renewal of part of the overhead power line from Walkmills to Bushmills with second-hand wire, poles, etc., obtained from the Antrim Electricity Distribution Company at the modest price of £7 13s. 9d.

Mr Keenan, the managing director and secretary, died during this period and Mr Chambers was requested to assist in the management of the Company.

The total number of passengers carried during 1935 was 98,351, an increase of 3,383 over 1934.

July and August 1936 produced a crop of minor mishaps. On 22nd July, motor-car Number 23 broke an axle, but was able to move to the nearest passing loop under its own power. In spite of the slight curtailment of the

Car No. 9 after the crude box was fitted (*c.* 1911) to shelter the crew .   *R. Wilkinson*

service due to this mishap, nearly 2,000 passengers were carried that day – almost a record! A spare pair of wheels and axle were fitted to Number 23 overnight and the car was in service again the next day.

Then on 24th July, car No. 9 failed due to a short-circuit in the trolley-standard. This again was rectified overnight. Just over a month later, on 25th August, occurred what might have been a serious accident. The tension bolt on the trolley of an unroofed electric car broke. Fortunately the trailer next to the electric car was roofed, and the boom struck this first, before falling on the head of a passenger, who had to have three stitches inserted in the resulting gash.

Presumably as a result of these mishaps it was decided to include in the winter programme, the fitting of roofs to the three electric cars not already so provided, namely cars Numbers 20, 21 and 22, and to advertise in the *Transport World* for second-hand cars. A decision was also taken that all cars not yet fitted for electric light be so fitted.

Mr Chambers was appointed manager and secretary of the Company in the autumn of 1936.

The winter of 1936-37 was a busy one, for not only were the above works on the rolling stock completed, but in addition, the track from Portrush railway station to the Methodist Church Curve was relaid at a cost of £200, and the passing loop at Portballintrae Road was shortened and raised to permit the County Council to widen the road junction. Half-a-mile of the track between Dunluce and Bushmills was raised, as the County Council decided to scarify and resurface the carriageway of the road, the material removed in the scarifying process again providing a convenient and cheap (probably free) supply of ballast for the tramway track.

In the early summer of 1937 the Company purchased a second-hand tramcar from the then recently closed Dunfermline and District Tramways system. The writer, holidaying at the Whiterocks in July 1937, well remembers the surprise he experienced when, on looking out of the window during lunch one day, he saw a Road Transport Board lorry and trailer, with a tramcar truck on the lorry and body on the trailer, slowly passing the bungalow. Subsequent investigation found the vehicles parked outside Portrush tram depot. The car was a single truck open-topped double-decker, in a rather faded and dingy all-green livery, and from recollection was Number 18 in the Dunfermline fleet. The destination 'Rumblingwell' on the car indicator struck a somewhat bizarre note. The car was purchased for £50 from Messrs. Alexander & Sons, Camelon, Falkirk, and 40 tons of tramway rails at £7 per ton from the same undertaking were also acquired.

During the winter of 1937-38 these rails were used to relay the tramway track in Causeway Street, Portrush, from the Methodist Church curve to the Gas Works, thus completing the relaying of the running track in the streets of Portrush. As the road surface was finished in tar-mac or asphalt, without stone setts along the rails, a very neat job was obtained, which lasted in good condition for the remainder of the life of the tramway.

Two other sections of track totalling one mile of the roadside tramway were also raised and re-sleepered.

The Dunfermline car, being 3 ft 6 in. gauge, had to have the wheels regauged to 3 ft and the body was converted to single deck by the simple process of removing the seats and duck-boarding from the top deck, making the deck waterproof with canvas, and providing a trolley plank and roof type trolley boom in place of the former upper deck pillar and boom. The end platforms were shortened and the step at one end altered so that entry to the car was from the same side at each end. Vestibules were provided at each end.

These modifications were carried out in Portrush depot during the winter of 1937-38 at a cost of £100, and the car entered service in June 1938, looking very smart in the Company's livery of cream and Tuscan red, with the number 24 above the driver's window at each end. Some

No. 24, ex-Dunfermline tram passing Portrush depot in 1946.   *D.G. Coakham*

difficulty was experienced at first with derailments due most probably to the longer wheel base and greater weight, compared to the existing cars, and also to the track being weak in places. However, by September, the engineer could report that:

> though trouble had been experienced at first in keeping the Dunfermline car on the track, the difficulty has been overcome and the car is now quite satisfactory in every respect.

Nevertheless, although Number 24 had roomy platforms, and was the only car in the fleet with rheostatic brake, it was never quite so popular with the men as Number 9, though it subsequently ran many miles and must have been a bargain at a total cost of only £195.

The weather during the summer of 1938 was not all that could be desired and passenger receipts reflected this by a considerable drop compared to 1937. Consequently, the maintenance programme for 1938-39 had to be curtailed, though at the request of the post office, condenser units were fitted to the six motor-cars to reduce radio interference.

There was a further drop in the number of passengers carried in 1939, probably due to the reluctance of people in Great Britain to go far afield on account of the mounting tension, culminating in the declaration of war on Sunday, 3rd September, 1939.

Motor-car No. 22 and original cars 6 (toast rack) and 1 (saloon) at Portrush station in 1934.
W. Robb

Chapter Ten

The Second World War and After

With the epic of Dunkirk, and the subsequent imminence of invasion in their minds, people had no thought for holidays, so in 1940, the total number of passengers carried dropped to just over 63,000.

The urgent need to accommodate and train the large numbers of troops, both British and Allied, evacuated from the beaches of Dunkirk, soon resulted in the establishment all over Northern Ireland of military camps and training centres, and one of the latter was located near the Giant's Causeway. In October 1940, the Commandant of this detachment approached the tramway company with. a view to the service being maintained throughout the winter. The Company agreed and ran a service but, quoting,

> received poor support from the Military, though the response from the general public was good, and a small profit was made on the additional expense.

This winter service, resumed in 1940, was re-introduced each winter for the next seven years. The working was based on Bushmills, and one car was sufficient to maintain the service throughout the day, apart from the first working (8.30 am) from Bushmills to Portrush which was arranged to suit people commencing work in Portrush around 9.00 or 9.15 am The car on this working remained at Portrush throughout the day, the crew being employed on maintenance work until they departed in it again at 5.20 pm for Bushmills. No. 24 frequently worked this turn.

The car which was to provide the service during the day ran unadvertised from Bushmills to the Giant's Causeway, to form the 10.15 am working thence to Portrush, and finished its day's work as the 6.00 pm Portrush to Bushmills, except on Thursdays and Saturdays, when it made two additional return journeys between Bushmills and Portrush, on which days the last working was the 9.30 pm Portrush to Bushmills.

Such a service involved only one scheduled crossing of cars per day, viz.: the 5.20 pm ex-Portrush and the 5.00 pm ex-the Causeway, so to reduce wear and tear on cars and track, at the end of each summer, the points at all passing loops were set for the straight road.

As all passing loops between Portrush and Bushmills were on the seaward side of the line, only the contact wire nearest the road was used by the trolley between those points, but between Bushmills and the Giant's Causeway the passing loops were on the landward side, so the seaward contact wire had to be used for that part of the journey. This meant that the conductor had to change the trolley from one contact wire to the other at Bushmills, otherwise an uncomfortable and, possibly an expensive, incident would have been experienced at the first passing loop beyond that station when the trolley tried to pass through the supporting standard located between the loop and the through line.

For the one scheduled crossing, or any others necessitated by special workings, the conductor on the car entering the loop had to change the trolley from one contact wire to the other while under way, then hold the points over to divert the car into the loop, and change the trolley back again on leaving the loop.

The air raids on Belfast in April and May 1941 resulted in the evacuation of many individuals, and several essential public services and their staffs, to the Portrush area, and this in turn produced a considerable improvement in tramway receipts for 1941-42.

The year 1942 saw the arrival of large detachments of United States Army, Navy and Air Forces in Northern Ireland, and during weekends and other leave periods, our American friends lived up to their reputation of being inveterate travellers, the railway stations at Belfast, Londonderry and other centres adjacent to United States establishments, being besieged on Saturdays and Sundays by G.I.'s, Doughboys and United States Marines, all anxious to purchase 'round trips' to any place the booking clerks cared to recommend. Consequently, most American servicemen stationed in Counties Antrim and Londonderry, eventually found themselves in Portrush where, on emerging from the station, they probably felt they were suffering from nostalgic delusions, as they saw what appeared to be a real live 'Toonerville Trolley' either parked at the sidewalk or approaching along Eglinton Street, and from 1942 onwards most trams, when the weather was reasonable, had their complement of Americans.

The American Red Cross, and the corresponding organizations for British and Allied Forces, also arranged tours for the troops and chartered special trams for the Portrush–Causeway journey, in fact on many occasions traffic necessitated all six motor-cars and their trailers being in operation simultaneously, so that the power stations were taxed to their limit and sometimes cars would only climb the inclines at walking pace. This was the signal for the more energetic of the G.I.s to drop off the cars and run alongside in good-humoured derision-a sprinter could easily abandon his seat on a trailer and join a 'buddy' on the motor-car at the 'head-end', and frequently availed himself of this facility.

THE SECOND WORLD WAR AND AFTER

Seen from the boarding side No. 9 passes Dunluce Castle. The bell and trolley hook are clearly seen above the front box. *Oakwood collection*

The re-introduction of a winter service in 1940, spurred the tramway company to provide electric heaters in motor-cars Numbers 9 and 24, which thus became two of the best-heated public road vehicles in the North of Ireland, as at that time heaters had been removed from the Belfast trams in the interests of fuel economy.

This unusual solicitude for passengers' comfort was justified by the financial results, which for the months October till March 1940-41, 1941-42, 1942-43, 1943-44 respectively were £.300, £460, £590, £912. At times the entire staff including the manager had to be put on to work as drivers or conductors.

Another gratifying feature was the phenomenal rise in the number of subscription tickets issued, 94 in 1940 and 1,689 in 1946. This was caused largely by the increased number of female workers travelling daily from Bushmills to Portrush to work in the hotels, boarding-houses, and cafes, which were kept busy 12 months per annum with Service personnel and employees of evacuated public services, etc.

The demands of war upon engineering labour and materials throughout Great Britain and Northern Ireland meant that the firms which normally carried out repairs or supplied materials were not available to the tramway during the war years, but the Company was fortunate enough to get two pairs of electric car wheels and axles and three pairs of trailer wheels and axles re-wheeled with chilled-iron wheels in Edinburgh in 1942, whilst Belfast Corporation Tramways undertook the repair of motor armatures. The acquisition of a power-operated drilling machine facilitated the manufacture of fish plates at Portrush depot, from bar stock.

The purchase of a bulk electricity supply from the Electricity Board for Northern Ireland and the operation of converting equipment was investigated in 1943, but was not considered to be advisable. The manager was then instructed to get information and prices for equipment to provide an additional electricity supply by means of water and diesel power.

The re-introduction of a winter service which on many occasions necessitated the use of the toast-rack motor-cars in addition to the two closed motors brought another development. Late in 1943 the manager arranged to have car Number 20 fitted with glazed ends for the protection of the drivers and passengers. Having inspected the prototype, the directors authorized the fitting of similar glazed ends to Number 23.

Two accidents occurred in the summer of 1944. On 23rd July, a driver had two fingers injured when jacking-up a derailed tramcar at Portrush depot, and one finger had to be amputated. Then on 6th August, a seven-year-old girl standing on the bank at the side of the track near Portrush slipped between the first and second trailers of an incoming tram and was killed.

In addition to the provision of glazed ends in cars Numbers 20 and 23, other works in 1944 included the complete re-wheeling of Number 24 and the fitting of one pair of new wheels to Number 9.

No. 20, with glazed ends, in the clearly defined trampath at Whiterocks.

Author's collection

THE SECOND WORLD WAR AND AFTER

A snowstorm on 20th January, 1945 formed drifts 18 in. to 24 in. deep across the tram track in many places, and service was suspended till 30th January. The turbines at Walkmills were also frozen solid.

Prior to 1945, one road of Bushmills Shed had not been provided with a trolley contact wire. Presumably this was a relic of the days when the steam engines were in use and the road in question was used for storing the passenger vehicles drawn by the steam engines. With the additional services operated during the war years, this road had to be used for an electric car and its trailers, and until 1945, the power to work this car in and out of the shed was obtained via a fairly long trailing cable which was clipped to the trolley head as required. This unsatisfactory method of operation ceased in 1945 when an overhead wire was provided to this road.

Another item of note about this period was the withdrawal of Number 9 from public view late in 1944 or early in 1945, and its re-emergence in June 1945 after a complete overhaul, with curved dashboards, glazed ends, ornamented side panels, and clerestory roof, a style of architecture absolutely unique, in which the Modern Functional Slightly Bulbous Streamlined School was tastefully blended with the original Victorian Ginger-Bread Gothic, and which, together with a complete repaint in the Company's livery of Tuscan red and cream, gave Number 9 a most attractive appearance.

The existing telephone instruments throughout the system were replaced with more up-to-date models.

During most of the summer of 1945 the water in the River Bush was at a low level and at times difficulty was experienced in getting the full output from the turbines.

Apart from the normal repairs and maintenance, during the winter of 1945-1946 Car Number 21 was given a complete overhaul and was fitted with glazed ends similar to those on Numbers 20 and 23.

Throughout the Second World War, the tramway had done yeoman service in maintaining an efficient transport service in its territory, running 50,000 or 60,000 miles per year, and, allowing for the respective carrying capacities of the trams and buses, probably saving 6,000 or 7,000 gallons of fuel oil per annum at a time when that commodity was in short supply. Nor did the services provided cater only for civilian needs or for the recreation and amusement of both civilians and members of the armed forces. On a number of occasions the Military Authorities chartered specials for the transport of troops between the camps in the vicinity of the Giant's Causeway and the railhead at Portrush, sometimes in the small hours of the morning, and residents along the route must have had eerie ideas about ghost trams, when disturbed from their slumbers at 3.00 am or 4.00 am by the rumble past their window of a tram laden with soldiery.

Damaged by enemy action in the First World War, the tramway suffered even more grievous bodily harm in the Second World War, though this was caused, not by the enemy, but by our own and Allied forces. At noon on 12th November, 1940 the cable of a drifting barrage balloon fouled the tramway overhead about 1¼ miles from the Portrush boundary and broke not only the wires but also the cross-arms of some of the poles, to the value of £48 14s., for which amount compensation was received in July 1941. Then on 17th December, 1942 a War Department vehicle collided with a pair of tramway poles at Stanalane passing loop near Bushmills. A wooden telegraph pole was substituted temporarily, but two second-hand steel poles were eventually obtained from Belfast Corporation Transport and a claim of £36 12s. 11d. was lodged against the War Department. Not to be outdone by their British Allies, the United States forces had a go at the tramway on 13th December, 1943, when one of their vehicles collided with a tramway standard in Causeway Street, Portrush, and broke it off at ground level. This cost the United States Authorities £22.

In the spring of 1946, the generator at Walkmills was given a complete overhaul, and the centre of the main dam was repaired with 1,000 bags of concrete.

The Portrush–Causeway fares were raised, single from 1s. to 1s. 2d. and return from 1s. 9d. to 2s. in time for the summer holiday traffic.

No. 9 after its 1945 rebuild, newly fitted with the body panels of car No. 3 and a handsome glass windshield replacing the box. *Oakwood collection*

THE SECOND WORLD WAR AND AFTER   79

An interesting sidelight during July was the lodging by a farmer of a claim against the Company for £35 damages in respect of a cow, which, he alleged, had escaped from her field through a gap in the roadside fence along the tramway, had travelled a considerable distance along the public road and then, doubtless in a moment of exhilaration caused by her unwonted freedom and forgetting the appropriate adage, leapt through a gap in the wall at the Gallery Curve, only to discover when it was too late to apply her brakes effectively, that the landing area on the other side of the wall was on a somewhat rocky seashore about 150 ft below her point of take-off. His claim was not successful as apparently the tramway company was not responsible for maintaining the fence along its roadside track, though in fact it had carried out repairs from time to time.

Normal maintenance in the winter of 1946-1947 must have been heavy, for the manager reported that due to pressure of work the fitting of glazed ends to Number 22 had to be deferred.

Fares were raised again at the beginning of July 1947, the Portrush–Giant's Causeway fare from 1s. 2d. to 1s. 6d. single and from 2s. 2d. to 2s. 6d. return, the Bushmills–Portrush 1s. day return being discontinued. It was decided not to employ a travelling ticket inspector, and the manager was instructed to carry out inspections at frequent but irregular intervals.

In September it was decided that, although receipts for the previous winter months had not been encouraging, a winter service would be operated till the end of December.

The track from Portrush depot to the Golf club house was in bad order, but heavier rails for relaying were not available at that time, so the joints were repacked to effect some improvement.

Information submitted in support of a proposal to raise the subscription ticket rates shows the very reasonable sum for which workpeople could travel between Bushmills and Portrush in 1947.

Existing rate (weekly)	2s.	Proposed	2s. 6d.
Existing rate (monthly)		Proposed	10s. 6d.

Ordinary Subscription Ticket Rates (New)

	Weekly	Monthly
Portrush to Golf Club	3s.	12s.
Portrush to Whiterocks	5s.	20s.
Portrush to Dunluce Castle	5s. 6d.	22s.
Portrush to Bushmills	6s.	24s.
Portrush to Giant's Causeway	7s. 6d.	30s.

Children under 14, half fare

From mid-August till 6th September the water level in the River Bush had been low, and the diesel engine at Portrush had to be used for longer periods than usual, to let water rise to a level which permitted efficient operation of the turbines.

As the other early electric tramway in Northern Ireland, the Bessbrook and Newry Tramway, was closing down, the manager of the Causeway line visited it to see if any of the rolling stock or equipment would be suitable for use on the latter. However, as most of the Bessbrook and Newry rolling stock was of the bogie variety, and as the electrical equipment was designed for operation at 250/300 volts, no purchases were made.

During the winter of 1947-48, car Number 20 was given a complete overhaul, and the repair facilities at Portrush depot were improved by the installation of an electric blower in place of the leather hand-bellows of the forge, and by the construction in the works of a travelling crane from old tram rails and a set of two-ton lifting blocks. A ton of iron bars was obtained for making fish plates.

For the first time since 1940, it was decided to suspend the tramway service from 27th December until the Monday before Easter. Furthermore, it was decided not to run a tramcar to convey the permanent way gang to and from their work. This obviated the necessity for an attendant at Walkmills power station. The service operated at Easter in 1948 and then was suspended from 1st April until the summer service was commenced on 1st May.

Early in 1948 the Government of Northern Ireland decided to form the Ulster Transport Authority to take over the operation of the Northern Ireland Road Transport Board, the Belfast & County Down Railway, and the railways of the former London Midland & Scottish (Northern Counties Committee). At a meeting in June of the tramway company's board, one of the directors suggested that the board should approach the newly-formed Authority and the Ministry of Commerce to ascertain whether the Authority would be interested in acquiring the tramway, as if so, this would relieve the Company of responsibility for reinstating the roadway if it decided to close down at some future date. His suggestion was adopted and another member of the board undertook to make the necessary enquiries. At a meeting of the board in September, it was reported that the Authority was not interested in acquiring the tramway.

Chapter Eleven

The Final Years

The engineer, Mr Chambers, had decided to resign at the end of September, and his report showed that the permanent way was in bad order, being wide to gauge in many places, many sleepers being almost entirely rotted away, and all points and crossing needing considerable attention. He also reported that the Jubilee Bridge over the River Bush was rapidly approaching a state in which it would no longer be safe for traffic. Car Number 24 required a new gear case and the platforms of two covered trailers required strengthening. Mr Chambers estimated that the wages necessary to carry out the works covered by his report would be about £1,000. Taking this amount and other expenses into account it was estimated that there would be a bank overdraft of some £650 by the end of April 1949.

Mr G. F. Meara was appointed as successor to Mr Chambers, to commence on 20th September, 1948. It had already been decided to suspend services from 30th September and the new manager was reminded of the obligation under the Company's Act, to run one tram per month, with conductor and money satchel, to avoid forfeiture of the track.

In his report of 30th November, 1948, the manager stated that the receipts for 1948 were £4,677 10s. 10d., the total number of passengers carried was 92,048, and the mileage run was 27,046. During October and November 104 yards of new rail had been laid on the line immediately on the Bushmills side of the Jubilee Bridge. On 15th October, lightning had struck the overhead cables and damaged the generator at Walkmills. As the Insurance Company was not liable, repairs were carried out by the tramway company.

He reported also that several sections of track were in a deplorable condition, particularly at curves and passing places. Two hundred second-hand sleepers had been received and 600 more were required. The directors congratulated Mr Meara on the amount of work he had carried out.

During the early part of 1949, three poles were filled with reinforced concrete, the timber decking of the Jubilee Bridge was repaired, the track at the Causeway Terminus and thence to Runkerry Siding was repaired, and from Runkerry Siding to Sandhills Siding the track was completely relaid, as was Dunluce Curve. All concrete sleepers had been removed as the rail fastenings had worked loose and it was impossible to tighten them. These sleepers could be re-used as kerbstones. The seaward rail on Clooney Hill had been raised and new sleepers inserted. These works had used up 16½ tons of rails previously purchased from the Bann Navigation and 1,100 sleepers. In addition to the above works, two points had been replaced and new lignum vitae blocks had been fitted on the internal bearings of the turbines at Walkmills.

Unfortunately, all the above work was largely in vain, for in November the manager had to report that the receipts for 1949 had dropped to £3,816 4s. 2d., the mileage run being 26,615. The tramway service had been discontinued from 30th September. The Ulster Transport Authority had written to the Company stating that, as the Government was not prepared to subsidise the undertaking, the Authority was not prepared to acquire it. Legal advice had been taken by the Company, and in the light of this, the directors felt that they had no alternative but to wind up the undertaking.

The manager stated that with the exception of the lady clerk in the office, one man in Portrush depot, and one man at Walkmills as caretaker, he had paid off all the staff on 15th October.

Even in its winding up, the Giant's Causeway Tramway had to be eccentric, for doubts arose as to whether application for the necessary Abandonment Order should be made under The Tramways Act (Ireland) 1860, or under The Transport Act (Northern Ireland) 1948, as part of it was a tramway and part a railway. Eventually, the Company had to be registered under the Companies Act (Northern Ireland) 1932 to avoid having to obtain a special Abandonment Act.

When the decision to wind up the Undertaking was made public in November 1949, protest letters appeared in all the local newspapers. Portrush Urban District Council, Antrim County Council, the Ulster Tourist Board, and other interested public bodies joined in an effort to avoid closure of the tramway.

At a meeting of the directors in August 1950, Mr Meara stated that, subject to the board's approval, he proposed to terminate his engagement as manager on 2nd September. This proposal was accepted, but to assist the public authorities interested in keeping the tramway open, he was asked to prepare an estimate of the cost of putting the tramway into good working condition. His estimate for this, including relaying the complete track with second-hand materials, renewing one trolley contact wire throughout, and overhauling the rolling stock, including the provision of air-brake equipment, was £14,600.

A deputation from the several authorities met representatives of the appropriate Government department on 22nd September, 1950, but the latter were not prepared to offer any assistance towards the preservation of the tramway as a working concern.

The Company, therefore, proceeded to obtain Abandonment Orders and realize its assets, but even this did not go without a hitch for, due to an oversight, the requisite number of public advertisements of the intention to apply for such orders, were not made, so that abandonment of the Bushmills–Causeway Section was delayed for seven months until September 1951.

However, arrangements were made to auction the track, overhead gear, power station equipment, rolling stock, etc., and this took place in Belfast on 15th March, 1951. The writer attended this, for a tramway enthusiast, rather melancholy function, and like many other interested people, was very surprised at the briskness of the bidding, the whole proceedings taking just over 35 minutes, and realising, in round figures, £11,000.

The principal items and prices realized were as follows:

9 miles 315 yards of track and 442 poles, together with approximately 600 yards of rails in stock	in situ	£7,250
16 miles of No. 1 s.w.g. copper wire (trolley)	in situ	
4 miles of No. 5 s.w.g. copper wire (o/h)	in situ	£2,700
8½ miles of No. 15 s.w.g. copper wire (telephone)	in situ	
2 closed and 4 open electric cars		
3 closed and 9 open trailer cars		£400
1 tower-wagon and 2 open wagons		
Turbines and generator at Walkmills		£160
Oil engine and generator at Portrush		£550
Paints, varnishes, etc.		£60
Blue moquette material		£20

In May 1951 the depot and ground at Portrush were sold for £2,800, and at an auction on 12th March, 1952 the buildings at the Causeway Terminus and 14 acres of land along the tramway were sold for £100; the Jubilee Bridge over the Bush realized £55; Bushmills station house and 1¾ acres fetched £860; and the wooden Car Sheds at Bushmills went for £200.

This ended the public life of the tramway, though the legal formalities dragged on during the following six years, until a Final Meeting of Creditors was called for 3.30 pm on 2nd September, 1958 and nobody turned up.

Portrush depot, where in August 1951, No. 24 (left) and 20 lie on wooden sleepers, their wheels, motors and electrical equipment stripped out and sold. A flat bed lorry sits on the right loaded with rails.
Oakwood collection

The scene at the Giant's Causeway terminus in August 1951, where lifted rails lie scattered after closure.
Oakwood collection

Appendix One

Steam Locomotives

The two steam locomotives Numbers 1 and 2 were of Messrs. Wilkinson's patent type, each carried on four 2 ft diameter solid wheels, the front and rear wheels being coupled by side rods. The wheel base was 5 ft 10½ in. A vertical boiler 5 ft high by 3 ft 8 in. diameter, fixed on the locomotive centre line but slightly nearer to one end of the machine than the other, supplied steam at 120 lb. per square inch to the launch-type engine which had two vertical cylinders each 7½ in. bore by 12 in. stroke. The cylinders and vertical engine frame were bolted to the boiler by a suitable saddle and the connecting rods drove downwards to the crankshaft, a pinion on which meshed with a gear wheel on one axle, the ratio being about 2 to 1. The geared drive made these engines good starters and pullers, but as the driven axle could not be sprung, they must have been rather hard on the track, and this is borne out by numerous references in the engineer's reports to the wear and tear on the track caused by working the goods traffic with these engines. Each engine weighed 7 tons and could pull a trailing load of 12 tons, or say, four or five loaded cars up an incline of 1 in 30.

The boilers were of the Field thimble-tube type, which gave good steaming. The exhaust steam from each cylinder first entered one of two receivers located one on each side of the boiler and then passed to a common superheating chamber of cast-iron, suspended in the upper part of the firebox, before being discharged to atmosphere via the blast pipe in the chimney. According to law, tramway locomotives were not supposed to have a noisy or visible exhaust and the receivers acted as silencers, whilst the superheater rendered the steam invisible when leaving the chimney. The engine prevented access to the boiler from one end, so the fire-door faced the other end. Coke was the fuel employed, and consumption was about 21 lb. per mile. When the driver was operating from the end at which the fire door was located, he was able to fire while on the move, if necessary, the fuel bunker being placed at this end of the locomotive, but when he was driving from the other end, he had to do his firing at stops, getting out and walking to the other end of the machine to do so. The water tank, presumably, was placed at the 'engine' end of the locomotive.

As the Board of Trade had placed a speed limit of 10 miles per hour on the tramway, each locomotive was fitted with an 'Allen's Paddle Type' governor, driven by belt or chain from a pulley on the axle. By suitable linkage, when the speed exceeded 10 miles per hour the governor operated a valve which admitted steam or water from the boiler to two small cylinders, one of which applied the brakes and the other put the engine into reverse gear.

Each locomotive, wheels and all, was enclosed in a sheet-steel casing extending from a few inches above rail level, to a height of about 5 ft A light metal canopy was provided to give the driver and machinery some protection from the rain, and lest the sight of the upper portion of the boiler should offend some critical passer-by or cause consternation to passing animals, two additional centre panels on each side were provided between the casing and the canopy. From old photographs of these engines, it would appear that these panels were originally glazed.

The effect of all this casing was to give the locomotives the general air of a couple of old ladies in crinolines, an effect rather heightened by the ornamental panelling and the fact that they were just about half as broad as they were long. As far as can be deduced from photographs, the engines were originally painted in the same livery as the cars.

As the water storage on the locomotives was of necessity rather restricted, lineside water tanks were provided at Portrush depot, Dunluce and Bushmills. These were rectangular iron tanks approximately 6 ft x 5 ft x 4 ft deep, holding about 650 gallons, and were supported about 9 ft above ground on timber frames.

Steam locomotive Number 3, delivered in 1886 and named *Dunluce Castle*, was basically similar to Numbers 1 and 2, but was somewhat longer and more powerful, being provided with cylinders 8 in. diameter x 12 in. stroke, and a boiler 6 ft x 3ft 8 in., pressed to 160 lb. per square inch.

The water tank was located behind the dashboard at the same end as the engine, the coke bunker being arranged in one corner of the opposite, or firing, end of the locomotive.

A regulator handle, similar to that of a railway locomotive, and a screw-down brake handle were provided at each end of the locomotive.

The overall length was about 12 ft and width 6 ft.

Locomotive Number 4, delivered in 1896, was practically identical to Number 3, and was named *Brian Boroimhe*, an example of Mr Traill's predilection for correctness of aristocratic detail, as the more plebeian rendering of the name was and is 'Brian Boru'.

Locomotive Number 2 was scrapped in 1898, but Number 1 survived until 1908 when it was dismantled. The boiler, machinery, and body were scrapped, but the body of one of the goods wagons was placed on the frame and wheels to form a permanent-way wagon and in this form it survived till the closure of the tramway.

Though Numbers 1, 2 and 3 were apparently originally painted cream and Tuscan red like the passenger vehicles, in later years Numbers 3 and 4 were painted green, from the writer's recollection Number 3 being a fairly dark privet green, whilst Number 4 was a somewhat lighter yellowish shade.

When the line was extended to the Giant's Causeway, water tanks were provided at the terminus and at the Causeway end of the Jubilee Bridge. They were rectangular tanks supported about 9 ft above ground level on timber supports as were those on the original part of the line.

Victoria Jubilee Bridge the rectangular water tank is visible on the left.

Oakwood collection

Appendix Two

Rolling Stock

Unfortunately for the historian, the tramway company did not keep any accurate records of rolling stock, probably due to the fact that it was chronically short of liquid capital; and new rolling stock in a number of instances, was purchased directly by Mr Traill, who was eventually paid by an issue of debentures or preference shares, and instructions to him from the board from time to time to acquire specific types of vehicle do not tally with the official annual rolling stock returns in several instances. Furthermore, although all vehicles were numbered from the beginning, fleet numbers were never quoted in minutes or reports during the first 20 or 30 years of the Company's existence. Fortunately, quite a number of photographs exist of scenes on the tramway in early days, and from these, together with the few reliable figures available, it has been possible to piece together the following account of the vehicles in use up till the introduction of the overhead trolley system; From then on, the problem was much simpler as more information regarding rolling stock was recorded.

The earliest reliable and reasonably detailed record of the vehicles possessed by the Company is that given at the time of the initial Board of Trade inspection in January 1883 viz.: 2 Wilkinson steam tram locomotives, 2 open first-class cars with motors, 2 closed first-class cars, 3 open third-class cars, together with some goods wagons and some tipping wagons. The first-class saloons were Numbers 1 and 2, the first-class open cars with motors were Numbers 3 and 4, and the open third-class cars were Numbers 5, 6 and 7.

Portrush looking towards the harbour. No. 3 *Dunluce Castle* moves to collect a pair of wagons and motor-car No. 4. *Ulster Museum, R.J. Welch collection*

In a paper read by Alexander Siemens and Dr. Edward Hopkinson, before the Society of Arts in London, in April 1883, it was stated that only one car had been fitted with a 'dynamo', but four other 'dynamos' were being constructed by Messrs. Siemens for delivery and installation in the cars before the summer season, two of the machines being large enough to draw a second car, so that 'seven cars would be available for traffic'.

The above information differs from the return of January 1883 in stating that only one car had been fitted with a motor, whilst the report stated that two cars were so fitted, but the total number of cars agrees, and even when the line closed in 1949, brackets of the type used to support the old motors were still in place under cars Numbers 2, 3, 4 and 7, though the presence of such brackets does not necessarily mean that a motor had ever been fitted, but only that provision had been made for installing a motor.

In the account of the opening ceremony in September 1883, the Viceregal party took their seats 'in the first of the *three* electric cars'. There is no doubt that Numbers 3 and 4 were two of these cars, but the third one could have been either Number 2 or Number 7. Photographs exist showing Number 7 operating as a motor-car, but none of the others, so it is a reasonable deduction that it was the third electric car at the opening ceremony, especially as in the account of that function, Numbers 1 and 2 were described as 'the two handsome saloon tramcars... drawn by a Wilkinson Steam Engine' and no mention was made of either being fitted with an electric motor.

Each motor-car had a single bi-polar Siemens motor of about 4 h.p. suspended under the floor, the drive from motor to axles being by means of roller chains. Reversal was by rocking the brush gear of the motor through the appropriate angle, a lever for the purpose being provided at the driving position at each end of the car. A handle on each end platform applied the brakes which were of the screw-down type employed in the normal railway brake-van, and acted on all four wheels. Two brake blocks per wheel were provided, probably to avoid putting excessive side thrust on the axle-box guides which were of light construction.

A speed of 12 mph could be attained on level track, and as the Board of Trade had imposed a 10 mph maximum, the cars were fitted. with a device designed by Mr E. B. Price, the tramway company's assistant engineer, which limited the speed to the statutory figure. This apparatus consisted essentially of a fly-weight governor and clutch-operated roller fitted to one axle of the car. A spring normally held the clutch in the disengaged position, allowing the roller to remain stationary whilst the axle rotated inside it. When the speed exceeded 10 mph, the centrifugal force acting on the governor weights became sufficient to overcome the spring of the clutch to which the governor was coupled by means of levers, and the clutch was engaged, causing the roller to rotate with the axle and wind up a chain connected to the brake rigging, thus applying the brakes until the speed of the car fell below 10 mph, when the brakes were automatically released. The date at which the apparatus fell into disuse is not recorded.

In one early description of the equipment, emphasis was laid on the fact that reversal of the motor provided a powerful brake. A car travelling at 15 mph stopped in little over its own length, but at the expense of breaking down the insulation on one of the field magnets. It was pointed out that such damage could be avoided by inserting a high resistance in circuit at the moment of reversal.

This was the germ of the rheostatic brake provided in later years on tramcars and trolley-buses.

Cars Numbers 1, 2, 3 and 4 were all of the same basic design, with elaborately panelled sides and open end-platforms. Numbers 1 and 2 were saloon cars with four windows per side and clerestory roofs. Numbers 3 and 4 were open cars, the bodies ending at the top of the side panels. Number 4, however, was provided with an awning roof supported on iron stanchions, and sometime later was provided with portable glass screens in wooden frames, which, when clamped to the roof stanchions, converted it to a closed car. Longitudinal seating with cushions for 18 or 20 passengers was provided in all these cars.

The car bodies were 15 ft long, and platforms 3 ft long, thus making the cars 21 ft long overall. The width was 5 ft 8 in. overall.

Cars Numbers 5, 6 and 7 were six-bench toast-racks, each bench seating 4 persons or 24 passengers per car, and were originally open at both sides and innocent of roofs. The length over bumpers was 18 ft 6 in. and width 5 ft 10 in.

The decision of the board in August 1883 (a month before the official opening) to order a first-class open electric car, two third-class open cars, a third-class covered car, a composite car, and two goods wagons, is rather confusing when considered in conjunction with the rolling stock return for December 1884, which was 4 electric cars, 6 trailers and 14 wagons, and a, statement by the engineer that all the vehicles ordered had been delivered and would be available for the summer traffic in 1885. Apparently only three passenger vehicles and two wagons had been ordered instead of the five passenger cars and two wagons decided upon in August 1883.

A possible, and in fact probable, explanation is that the ordering of a first-class open electric car only referred to the fitting of a motor to Number 3 or Number 4, and that the third-class covered car was obtained by fitting a roof and sides to Number 7. Of the three additional cars, Number 8 was definitely a six-bench toast-rack similar to Numbers 5, 6 and 7 and Number 10 was a five-bench toast-rack. No definite information is known regarding Number 9, though the description 'composite car' suggests the saloon electric car which bore that number in later years, but there are reasons for believing that this saloon did not arrive for some years, the principal one being that it was of similar construction to the second Number 10. As there are several photographs showing toast-rack Number 10 in service after the Causeway Extension had been opened in 1887, it is improbable that Saloon Number 10 arrived before that year, and Saloon Number 9 was most likely delivered about the same time, say between 1888 and 1890.

Trailer cars Nos. 1, 10, 8 and 2 at the Giant's Causeway terminus about 1890.
National Library of Ireland W. Lawrence collection

No. 11 at the rear of a train at the Portrush terminus, June 1948.

Oakwood collection

The board's decision in January 1888 to order three light open trailers, one large open electric car, two full-size open trailers and six open goods wagons appears to have been another example of wishful thinking, as the nett result was the conversion of five goods wagons to small five-bench trailers, presumably Numbers 11 to 15 inclusive, with a corresponding reduction in the number of wagons from 14 to nine.

Then in 1891 two more wagons were converted into passenger vehicles, presumably Numbers 16 and 17.

As mentioned later, Numbers 11, 13, 15 and 16, survived in service until the closure of the line and could be easily identified as conversions from goods wagons.

In view of the publicity given to the excellencies of the original saloon vehicles, which with becoming modesty were described as 'perfect models of good taste, comfort, and lightness', the unobtrusive entry into service of saloons Numbers 9 and 10 is hard to understand.

As will be seen from the illustrations, these two vehicles were basically similar in design to the original saloons Numbers 1 and 2, except that the side panels were plain, whereas the sides of the older cars were highly ornamental, being divided into 12 small arched panels and a large rectangular central panel enclosing an oval panel within which the Company's seal was reproduced in colour. The older cars also had four windows per side, the two central windows each being 3 ft 11 in. wide, the width of each end window being 2 ft 10 in.

The bodies of Numbers 9 and 10 were 15 ft 6 in. long, the platforms being 2 ft 4½ in. long, giving a length of 20 ft 3 in. against the 21 ft of Numbers 1, 2, 3 and 4. Normal longitudinal seating was provided in all six cars.

The newer cars each had seven windows per side, those on Number 10 being equal in size. Number 9, however, must have been unique, as the two windows at one end were each 2 ft 3in. wide, whilst the remaining five were 2 ft wide. The reason for this unusual

No. 9 in 1949 at the Giant's Causeway terminus.   *Author*

window arrangement was that Number 9 was divided into 'First' and 'Ordinary' class with a partition, complete with sliding door, between the two sections. The two larger windows at the one end allowed the first-class portion to be made 4 ft 6 in. long, seating six persons, without the partition having to be located in the glass portion of the third window, which would have been the case, had all the windows been of equal width. The seats in the first-class portion were provided with cushions and curtains adorned the windows. Passengers in the 'Ordinary' portion had to be content with slatted seats and uncurtained windows, and be able to accommodate the seating portion of their anatomy in either 1 ft 5½ in. or 1 ft 3 in. of seat, according to the state of trade, whilst the fortunate possessors of first-class tickets could lounge at ease in at least 1 ft 6 in. of seating space, their complexions protected from the ravages of the sun's rays by the tasteful draperies, and their dignity by a large notice stating in full and unequivocally, 'First Class Compartment'. All these amenities survived the conversion of Number 9 for operation on the overhead system, until the abolition of first class in 1923.

After the conversion of the two wagons into passenger cars in 1891, the rolling stock remained at 4 electric cars, 13 trailers, and 7 wagons until the acquisition of Numbers 18 and 19 in 1897. These were seven-bench toast-rack trailers, each seating 28 passengers, and were open at one side only, as were all the toast-racks from, and including, the original Number 10.

The earlier toast-rack cars Numbers 5, 6 and 7 eventually had the gaps between the seat ends on the side next to the hedge filled in with wooden panels, but Number 8 remained open at both sides until scrapped in the 1920s.

Twelve goods vehicles were originally provided, though whether this number included Mr Geogechan's patent tipping wagons was not specifically stated, but it is almost certain that there were six goods wagons and six tipping wagons. This assumption is supported by the ordering in December 1882 of six tarpaulins, 16 ft. x 11 ft 6 in., at 1s. 8d. per square yard 'to cover the trucks?', and by a statement in 1917 that '6 tip wagons went to scrap'.

From photographs, the tipping wagons were steel hoppers arranged for side tipping, similar to those still in use on constructional railways, but very much larger.

The goods wagons were exactly similar to the passenger cars Numbers 1 to 4 up to floor level, but were provided with drop-ends and sides, two planks high. A brake handle was provided at one end only, and the overall length was about 15 ft.

The cars and wagons were coupled together as required by means of draw bars about 4 ft long formed with a forked eye at each end. Under the floor, at each end of each vehicle, spring-loaded draw-gear with a single eye was fitted. The double eye of the draw bar fitted over the single eye on the draw-gear, on which it was retained by a vertical steel pin. A single safety chain with hook was also provided at each end as a second line of defence against a break-away.

When a motor-car working with a trailer reached a terminus the conductor had to unhook the safety chains, pull the pins in the draw-gear and transfer about a quarter of a hundredweight of drawbar to the other end of the trailer, for recoupling for the return journey.

The wheel base of all the original cars and goods wagons was 6 ft 6 in.

Spring buffers were not fitted, a single, iron-bound wooden bumping block on the centre line at each end of the vehicles being all that was considered necessary for this purpose.

The livery, as far as can be determined from contemporary photographs, was similar to that obtaining at the closure of the line, viz.: cream panels with the ornamental beading between panels, the rocker panels on Numbers 1, 2, 3 and 4, and general lining, painted Tuscan red. On some of the cars the dark portions approximated to a chocolate colour, but this may have been due to fading.

The rolling stock return for the end of 1898 included 4 electric cars and 15 trailers, a total of 19 passenger vehicles, and as the two new toast-rack type electric cars obtained for the inauguration of the overhead system in July 1899 were numbered 20 and 21, it can be safely assumed that the numbers ran consecutively without any blanks, especially as the return at the end of 1889 gave 4 electric cars and 17 trailers.

The return of four electric cars for the end of 1899, when only two new electric cars had been purchased, raises the intriguing question as to which of the four old electric cars were converted for working on the overhead system.

Each of the two new cars had a seven-bench toast-rack body mounted on a Peckham truck with the normal two-motor equipment, though, as the voltage was probably only 250 or 300 volts during the first year of operation (see the section on Walkmills power station), the cars must have been operated with only one motor switched in at a time, or with the travel of the controller handle limited to the parallel notches only. The first method is the more likely one to have been adopted, as it only required the operation of the reversing lever. Thompson-Houston Controllers of a model in which the handle was moved through a complete circle (less the thickness of the stop) to obtain full power were provided at each end of each car. Trolley-heads were of the swivelling type, and each trolley-boom was supported on the normal floor-mounted, cast-iron, pillar-like standard of the period, with two large helical springs arranged externally to keep the trolley in contact with the

ROLLING STOCK 93

No. 21 leaving Portrush, May 1920.   *Oakwood collection*

overhead wire. As neither vehicle had a roof, the external springs presented no problem. Only Number 3 of the old-type electric cars was roofless, so that logically it was the one most likely to be converted. Nevertheless, a careful examination of this car about 1950 failed to reveal any traces of conversion having been attempted.

An examination of Number 4, however, showed that a hole had been cut in the roof to accommodate a trolley standard and the position of the base of the standard and its fixing bolts was quite clearly apparent on the floor.

The rolling stock return at the end of 1900 included only 3 electric cars but 18 trailers, so that one car had been 'de-electrified'.

The most logical explanation of this is that two of the original electric cars were returned as such at the end of 1899, though not suitable for operating on the overhead system, then Number 4 was converted experimentally, and the motor of the other old car scrapped.

The next addition to the rolling stock was the car put into service in 1902. Like Numbers 20 and 21, this car was a seven-bench toast-rack on a Peckham truck.

As the rolling stock return at the end of 1902 included only 3 electric cars but 19 trailers, the career of Number 4 as an electric car apparently came to an end in 1902.

Number 4 could accommodate only one motor, and that of the old-fashioned type, so operation could not have been very satisfactory once the supply voltage was raised to 550 volts.

Six years passed before the next electric car, Number 23, commenced running in 1908. This was the car which was built in place of the car which did not arrive from America, and was again a seven-bench toast-rack, the body being identical with those of Numbers 20, 21 and 22, but with the addition of a wooden roof of awning type supported on iron stanchions.

Unlike the three existing cars, Number 23 was mounted on a United Electric Car Company's Patent Suspension Truck of a type in which the load was transmitted from the truck frame to each axle box through two half-elliptical springs arranged one above and one below the box.

Another Peckham truck was purchased cheap in 1908 from the Malleable Steel Casting Co., Pendleton, for the modest sum of £30. This could hardly have included motors, and a subsequent entry of £122 2s. 'for an additional motor and controller for the new electric car' suggests that an existing motor and controller were being pressed into service. These may of course have been spares for the existing cars, but it is possible that they were those used on Number 4 during its short and not entirely satisfactory career as an overhead electric car, possibly with a single controller amidships.

At any rate, in 1909 the body of Number 9 was placed on the new truck, with a consequent rise in the number of electric cars to five, and a drop in the number of trailers to 18, figures which remained constant for many years.

The body work of Number 9 had not been constructed to support a trolley-boom mounted on the roof, so a cast-iron standard similar to those on the toast-racks was bolted to the floor at the mid-point of one side, a hole being cut in the roof through which the top of the standard projected, to support the trolley-boom. This avoided any strain on the bodywork and roof, but the metamorphosis admittedly reduced the accommodation available to the 'Ordinary' passengers by the diameter of the trolley standard. This reduction in space was somewhat compensated, however, by the two additional 'comer seats' provided by the aforementioned trolley standard.

After Number 9 had been in service for a year or two in this guise, some additional modifications were made to protect the driver and conductor from the elements. A rather crude box-like structure was added between the top of the dashboard and the underside of the roof at each end of the car. An opening 20 in. high by 16 in. wide, fitted with a hinged and glazed door, was provided to give the driver a view of the road and the conductor access to the trolley rope. A bell of fire-engine variety, was fixed on the platform roof at each end. These bells were probably relics from one of the first steam locomotives. A leathern thong from the clapper descending through a hole in the canopy roof allowed the driver to give very audible warning of his approach, the conductor to make the necessary platform signals, and Number 9 to bounce over defective rail joints and jerk round curves or points to a gentle musical tintinnabulation suggestive of leprechauns.

At each end of the roof a large hook was fixed, under which the conductor could fix the trolley-boom when coasting down hill.

All five cars were provided with these hooks, Number 23 having them fixed to the ends of its roof like Number 9. As Numbers 20, 21 and 22 had no roofs, a wooden post about 2½ in. square and 7 ft high was fixed at the centre of each dashboard to carry the trolley hook.

The trolley standards on all cars were located as closely as
possible to the sea-side of the cars, and a spring-loaded reel was provided on the end of each trolley rope to keep the latter taut, a bayonet-type socket for holding the reel being fixed on the outside of each dashboard.

The trucks of all five cars had a wheel-base of 7 ft, the wheel diameter being 2 ft 6 in. Each car had two 19.5 h.p. motors and could easily draw two trailers.

After the conversion of Number 9 in 1909, no new rolling stock was added until the purchase in 1937 of the car from the Dunfermline and District Tramways, already described, the truck of which was again a Peckham, but this time of the pendulum variety, provided with two 25 h.p. motors.

ROLLING STOCK

No. 23 passing the town hall in Portrush. The ornamental cast-iron base that graced the tram wire supports in the streets of Portrush is easily seen on the left. *Oakwood collection*

No. 9 resting in the sidings at the Causeway terminus, 10th August, 1930. *Oakwood collection*

Motor car No.22 and the tower wagon in 1947. *Author*

No. 22 sporting a new roof fitted in 1934 (*page* 72 shows it before it was rebuilt) passing Whiterocks loop in 1937. Note the old third rail still in place as a fence. *W. Robb*

The only item of rolling stock not yet described is the tower wagon. This vehicle strongly resembled a medieval engine of siege warfare, and a horse which shied at it in 1905 had some justification for its behaviour. It consisted basically of four wooden stanchions, arranged in a slightly pyramidal fashion, to support a working platform approximately 11 ft above rail level. Slats fixed across the supporting timbers' at one end provided a ladder giving access to the working platform, which was protected by a wooden handrail and wooden sheeting. This erection was mounted on one of the goods wagons and so far generally resembled the tower wagons of the Manx Electric Railway. It surpassed the latter, however, in having incorporated in its superstructure a sort of mobile blacksmith's shop cum workshop, formed by boarding between the supporting timbers and cladding the lot in roofing-felt. The portable forge had, of course, to be lifted into the open before lighting up. The tower wagon was usually accompanied by an open truck, which consisted of an old wagon body mounted on the underframe and wheels of one of the first pair of steam locomotives. Motive power was supplied almost invariably by Toast-rack Number 22, and the presiding genius of this convoy was Bob Scott, who had worked on the Tramway from boyhood in all capacities, and who for the last 30 years of its existence was general maintenance man. His rotund figure and large walrus moustache, excelled only by that of Bairnsfather's 'Old Bill', could be seen one day soldering a supporting ear to the overhead or applying a liberal coating of tar to the Jubilee Bridge, and the next day (or maybe later in the same day) replacing a defective fishplate in the track, or acting as driver on an 'extra' tram. He survived the tramway by only three years as he died at Bushmills on 18th December, 1952.

When the tramway ceased operation in September 1949 the rolling stock existing was as follows:

    Electric Cars:
        Saloons — Numbers 9, 24;
        Open Toast-racks — Numbers 20, 21, 22, 23.

    Trailer Cars:
        Saloons — Numbers 1, 2, 10;
        Open (longitudinal seats) — Numbers 3, 4;
        Open (toast-rack) — Numbers 5, 6, 7, 11, 13, 15, 16, 19.

Number 3 had not been in use for years, and the side panels had been stripped from it in 1945 and used in rebuilding Number 9. Though the body of Number 9 was 6 in. longer than that of Number 3, this was neatly and unobtrusively overcome by adding 3 in. of plain panel at each end.

The cars converted from goods vehicles, i.e. Numbers 11, 13, 15 and 16 could be easily identified as they were of the five-bench variety, appeared to have double floors as the bodies had been set on the original wagon floors, and had a brake handle at only one end.

In later years all the toast-rack cars and Number 4 were provided with side tarpaulins. These were permanently fixed along the edges of the roofs of the cars throughout the entire length of the vehicles, a wooden batten of similar length being fixed along the free, or bottom, edge of each tarpaulin, which in the unfurled position just met the top edges of the seats. Short pieces of rope fixed to each batten were secured to the lower ends of the roof stanchions to keep the tarpaulins from waving in the breeze when unfurled to protect the passengers from wind and rain. When not required, each tarpaulin was rolled up on its batten, like a giant roller blind in reverse, and secured along the edge of the roof by several canvas straps provided for that purpose.

As far as possible, a saloon car was included in each rake of vehicles, except during settled fine weather.

This completes the description of the rolling stock as far as information is available, but the following note may be of some interest.

In a 'hand-out' to the Press in 1882, it was stated that 'the tramcars and wagons are being built to special designs... and these will also be fitted with separate 'dynamos' and secondary batteries.'

From this it appears that the original intention was to have a motor on each vehicle with multiple unit control, and to work through the streets of Portrush and Bushmills by accumulator power, which was then being tried out in England and on the Continent. No evidence of accumulator use exists, but one of the illustrations on another page shows a goods wagon with motor brackets fitted (*see page* 26). Car Number 15, an obvious conversion from a goods wagon, had such brackets under it at the time of closure.

Cars at Portrush depot stripped and waiting for the scrap yard, August 1951.

Oakwood collection

Appendix Three

Walkmills Hydro-Electric Power Station

Walkmills power station was situated about 300 yards from the Coleraine Road, at the Salmon Leap, and was a single storey masonry building, rectangular in plan and measuring about 30 ft x 25 ft, built at the side of the head race which terminated in a large timber tank roughly 20 ft long, 9 ft wide and 8 ft deep, supported on beams spanning the recess which had been blasted out of the cliff face to accommodate the turbines.

From the 'floor' of the tank two 3 ft 6 in. diameter steel penstocks extended almost vertically downwards, to each turbine. These were of the vertical shaft type, and the original machines, manufactured by Messrs. Allcott & Co., of New York, were each of 45

Exterior of Walkmills Hydro-Electric Power Station, probably soon after opening.
Ulster Museum, R.J. Welch collection

h.p., giving a total of 90 h.p. The shafts extended upwards just outside the tank to above the water level and, by means of bevel gearing, transmitted their motion to two horizontal shafts arranged across the top of the supply tank. These two shafts were coupled by means of spur gearing to a third shaft which extended through the wall of the power house, inside which a combined clutch-pulley was fitted on the shaft. From the pulley the dynamo, a Siemens bi-polar machine of about 40 h.p., was driven by means of a flat belt. Each turbine incorporated a 'gate' by which the quantity of water admitted to the runner could be controlled. As the movement of the gates was vertical, presumably the turbines were of the Fourneyron type.

By means of a system of levers and chains, terminating in two hand-wheels located inside the power house, the position of the turbine gates could be adjusted to suit the varying load. With the intention of avoiding the necessity for constantly altering the gate setting manually, a governor was provided to do this automatically. This apparatus was of the type on which a small framework supporting two pawls was, by a suitable drive from the turbine shaft, oscillated around a pawl wheel connected to the controls of the turbine gates, so that rotation of the wheel in one direction opened the gates, and rotation in the other direction closed them. Each pawl tended to turn the pawl-wheel in opposite directions, and if both could bear on the wheel it also would have merely oscillated. A shroud which extended over a segment of the pawl wheel was, therefore, provided between the wheel and the pawls. An ordinary fly-weight governor, by a system of levers controlled the position of this shroud, so that if the turbine speed was too high, only the pawl which would move the pawl wheel in the direction for closing the turbine gate would be allowed to engage the wheel, until the speed had fallen to normal, when the shroud would be moved to a position which prevented both pawls from engaging. If the speed was sub-normal, the other pawl would be allowed to operate, and so on.

The interior of the power station in 1932. *Author*

This type of governor is inherently sluggish in operation, and would have been unsuitable for the rapidly varying load produced by one or more tramcars stopping or starting frequently, and doubtless its use was discontinued at an early date, in favour of manual control.

In addition to the turbine control described in the foregoing paragraphs, a friction clutch was provided on each of the horizontal shafts from the turbines, so that either turbine could be disconnected from the common drive, for purposes of repair or water economy when the river was low. The clutch pulley on the main shaft driving the dynamo, permitted the latter to be instantly disconnected from the turbines in case of accident.

To permit either turbine being dismantled whilst the other continued in service, a flap-valve was provided in each opening where the penstocks left the bottom of the wooden tank.

As already stated, the head-race was 9 ft wide by 8 ft deep, and extended upstream from the power station for about 200 yards to the point where a weir 180 ft long extended at an angle across the River Bush, increasing the depth of water by five or six feet for almost two miles upstream thus providing a potential draw-off of the order of three million cubic feet.

With the 26 ft drop available at the turbines and allowing an efficiency of about 50 per cent, the impounded water represented about 1,500 horsepower hours, or, say, ten hours' continuous operation, if the whole natural flow of the river were allowed to pass over the Salmon Leap, and thus be lost to the turbines.

In actual practice, even under minimum flow conditions, the storage provided by the weir permitted several hours' operation of the plant per day.

It will be recollected that the chairman's speech at the half-yearly meeting in August 1884 mentioned that 'the first machines they had were now only fit for museums, and had been returned to Siemens for modernization'. When they were received back in due course, the Company alleged that they were useless, and some acrimonious correspondence ensued. It is possible that a coolness may have arisen consequently between the parties and this may account for the fact that the second generator installed in Walkmills in 1887 was supplied by Messrs. Ellwell Parker.

Once the larger generator was in commission, the original one at Walkmills, and the small one at Portrush were taken out of service and the bits and pieces reassembled in some way to produce one machine which was eventually reinstalled about 1891 or 1892 in Walkmills beside the Ellwell Parker machine and remained in position for more than 30 years.

The next major alteration to the generating equipment in Walkmills power station, was the replacement of the Ellwell Parker machine by a new generator from the Electric Construction Company in 1900 or 1901, after the overhead system had been initiated.

From this it would appear that for at least the first year of operation on the overhead system, the voltage remained at the nominal 250 volts used with the original side contact rail system though of course it could have been run at the 300 volts noted by Major Cardew in 1895.

This would also explain how two of the original motor-cars could have been used for a year or so on the overhead system. It would only have been necessary to fit them with trolleys in place of the old pick-up brushes or shoes.

Then in 1907 the final generator in Walkmills was installed. This was also an Electric Construction Company production, and was rated to give 180 amps. at 550 volts, an output of 130 h.p., and continued to do so until the closing of the tramway in 1949.

This machine ran for over 20 years without repair, or, according to the power station attendant, without having the commutator skimmed, the only attention given to it being the filling of the hearings with oil every Easter Monday.

As recorded elsewhere, one new turbine was obtained from Messrs. Turnbull in 1900, and another in 1903, and these also lasted until the end. They were reputed to he of 75 h.p. and 50 h.p. which is rather less than the rating of the generator, a somewhat unusual arrangement, but it is possible that they were available at bargain prices.

An unusual and unofficial adjunct to the electrical equipment was a knife switch conveniently located beside the operator as he sat at the controls so that, having placed an unlighted cigarette between his lips, he had only to strike an arc between the switch contacts, then lean over and ignite the weed thereat.

Another one was a home-made wooden cage which was anchored a short distance upstream in the head-race, and which formed a convenient repository for any eels which the power station staff might have been lucky enough to ensnare in the race.

For many years the Walkmills plant was in the charge of one Robert Maxwell, and when he died in 1943 at the age of 79, the Company had fixed to the wall of the plant room in which he had spent so much of his working life, a brass memorial tablet on which was engraved 'To remind you of Bob Maxwell, 1864-1943, for 57 years operational and maintenance engineer of this hydroelectric generating station.'

Looking upstream on the River Bush to the waterfalls that provided the drop for the power station, 13th July, 1933. *Oakwood collection*

Appendix Four

The Overhead System

The overhead system was of the side pole and bracket type. The poles were about 18 ft high, the lower portion up to about 8 ft 6 in. above ground level being 6 in. diameter, and the upper portion 4¾ in. diameter. The bracket arms and struts were 1½ in. diameter. The struts were at 45° to the horizontal and the length of the strut was varied to suit the length of the bracket arm. At places where a bracket length exceeding about 7 ft was required, e.g. at passing loops, two poles with a crossbar, or crossbar and bracket, were used. The Company's telephone wires were carried on normal insulators mounted on the tops of the poles or on short rearward extensions of the bracket arms.

The supporting ears of the overhead contact wires were fixed rigidly to the bracket arms by means of shed-type insulators, multiple disc insulators being provided on the arms to improve the insulation from earth.

This type of rigid fixing, combined with a fair amount of slack in the contact wires, was conducive to trolley bounce and consequent arcing at each support, which in turn tended to cause the contact wire to break at these points, so stirrup wires supported from insulators mounted on the upper side of each bracket arm were provided to prevent the live contact wire from falling to the ground in case of breakage.

The idea of providing these stirrup wires was that of Dr. Hopkinson, who devised it about 1895 or 1896 to deal with similar breakages on the Manx Electric Railway, for which he was electrical engineering consultant.

Feeder points were provided at Portrush depot, the Whiterocks, Dunluce, Bushmills, and Giant's Causeway. At Dunluce was located a switch-house constructed of old railway sleepers, tarred and felted, and resembling a railway platelayer's hut. This housed the switch-gear necessary to isolate the overhead system into two separate parts at times of heavy load when the diesel-driven generator at Portrush and the turbine-driven generator at Walkmills were both working. The characteristics of these machines were such that they could not operate satisfactorily in parallel, so the Portrush generator served the line as far as Dunluce and the Walkmills generator served the portion from Dunluce to the Giant's Causeway.

The Walkmills generator was usually adequate to deal with the load of the entire system before lunch time and after about 7 pm, the peak load occurring in the afternoon. The necessary switching at Dunluce was carried out by the conductor of a specified tram, and to help him to avoid operating the switch when current was passing through it, a bank of lamps, and a telephone communicating with the power stations, were provided in the hut along with the necessary switch-gear.

On arrival at Dunluce, the designated conductor would unlock the hut, notify the power stations by telephone of his arrival, and switch on the bank of lamps. The two power station operators would then adjust their respective generators until the voltages in the two sections meeting at Dunluce were identical. When this occurred the lamps would cease to glow and the conductor then operated the switch as required, switched off the bank of lamps, completed his telephoning, locked the door of the hut, and departed on his tram.

By the time the overhead system had been in use for 15 or 20 years, and in spite of liberal applications of tar to the poles and fittings, the corrosive effect of the salt-laden sea breezes on some of these was becoming serious. Funds were not available for the purchase of replacements, so when a pole was obviously in a delicate state of health, the maintenance branch had no option but to operate. The head of the pole was removed, three or four ½ in. or ⅝ in. steel bars, suitably spaced, were inserted throughout its length, and concrete was then poured in and rammed home until the inside of the pole was solid reinforced concrete. When the head was replaced, the pole was as good as, or better than when new. By the time the tramway closed down, most of the poles had been treated in this way, and their removal caused the demolition men quite a lot of unexpected hard work.

In the streets of Portrush, the poles were painted a dark, reddish brown, and were originally provided with ornamental cast-iron plinths, some of which survived until the end, and were still in place when the 1963 edition of this book was published.

The overhead power line from Walkmills to Bushmills was of unique construction for a power line. At first glance it looked like an ordinary telegraph line, the supports being ordinary telegraph poles with crossbars and normal shed-type insulators, though the poles were rather shorter than the normal pole. A more careful inspection, however, revealed that there were only five conductors, that these were much heavier than telegraph or telephone wires, and that midway between each pair of poles the wires were bound together and soldered, creating the effect of rays of light coming to a focus and then separating again.

Each conductor was a No. 5 s.w.g. solid copper wire (standard wire guage, No. 5 is 0.212 in. 5.385 mm thick), and the binding together of these between each pair of poles ensured uniform electrical loading and reduced swinging when a wind was blowing.

The return cable was underground, probably the original cable with the cores bonded at intervals.

Bushmills station showing the overhead system there. *Oakwood collection*

Appendix Five

Portrush Depot

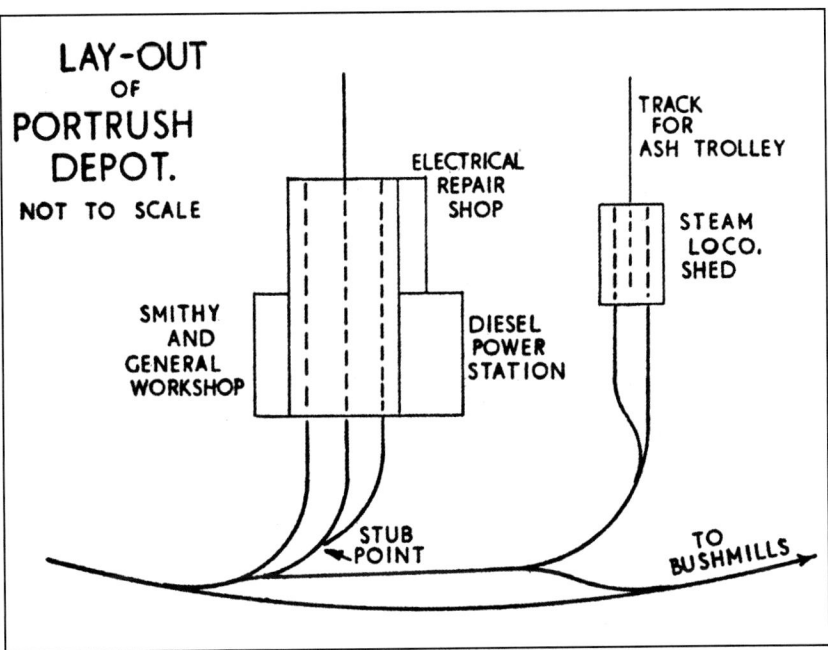

Portrush depot was a solidly constructed building, the walls being of random rubble masonry in black basalt, with a pitched roof of slate. The window and door openings and corners were executed in white glazed brick, the general effect being quite pleasant.

Referring to the drawing, the workshop and smithy were located in the bay behind the window on the left, the three storage roads were of course behind the three high doors, and the bay with the three windows and the curved roof was the diesel driven power station erected in 1925.

About 50 ft to the right, and not shown on the sketch, was the two-road wooden shed, used to stable the steam locomotives.

The depot could accommodate 18 cars, and the loco shed was large enough to house the four steam engines.

The centre road of the depot was not provided with an overhead contact wire, so was used principally for trailer cars which could be hand-shunted easily by two men, though of course motorcars could be worked into it, using a trailing lead.

An antiquarian item which survived until the end of the tramway was the stub point used to divert cars to the centre road or the road next to the diesel power station, as required.

The building became a petrol filling station, initially the original frontage was covered by a modern stucco and teak facade, but after modernization of the filling station, the original buildings have been demolished.

Driver Robert Sharp stands in the cab of No. 21 at Portrush depot. *Oakwood collection*

The tram sheds at Bushmills. *Author's collection*

Appendix Six

Tickets And Fares

The fares charged at the opening of the line in 1883 have been quoted in the section describing that period of the line's history, and as already mentioned, there were two classes available, 'First Class Car' and 'Ordinary Car', the first-class fare being from 25% to 100% dearer than the ordinary fare, and return fares being from 50% to 100% dearer than the corresponding single fares according to what the traffic might be expected to bear.

The Railway Company also booked passengers from certain stations, e.g. Belfast, right through to the Giant's Causeway and continued to do so throughout the life of the tramway.

In 1923 First Class was abolished on the tramway but tickets continued to be designated 'Ordinary Car'.

There were about 12 different tickets in use, those for single journeys being printed on heavy paper or light card of the type used by most tramway systems, but were not marked in stages. They all bore the description of the journey or journeys for which they were available, in the form:

> Portrush to Ballymoney Road,
> or Giant's Causeway to Bushmills
> or vice versa.
> Available for one journey only.
> Ordinary Car.   Fare 4*d*.
> Not transferable.

and were numbered sequentially with an index letter and a four digit number in the normal way.

The return tickets were of the same size, and printed on the same heavy card, as the normal railway ticket. With one exception, they were printed in the same form as a return railway ticket, and were indented between the two halves to facilitate division, though of course neither half was overprinted with an 'R', as the direction of the original journey determined which half was the return.

The exception to the above arrangement was the Portrush Portballintrae return, which was of the same size, and on the same heavy card as the other return tickets, but was worded on the 'vice versa' principle, i.e.

> Portrush to
> Port Ballintrae
> and back or vice versa.

and was not arranged for division. There is no obvious reason why this special treatment should have been accorded to this particular journey.

One other return ticket, that for Dunluce Castle, had unusual wording. This ticket was arranged for division in the usual way but the wording of the respective halves was:

> Dunluce Castle   :   Portrush or
> to Bushmills   :   Bushmills to
> or Portrush   :   Dunluce Castle

The reverse side of all single and return tickets for at least a quarter of a century and possibly much longer, bore the same advertisement for the same Portrush emporium: 'When at Portrush visit the White House'.

The accompanying table (*on the facing page*) summarises the ticket situation as regards type, colour, and fares, though there were certain special tickets such as the 1s. return, Portrush to Giant's Causeway, for HM and Allied Forces, which are not included.

Return tickets could be obtained if desired from the Portrush office, and up till 1939 or 1940, from the offices at Bushmills and the Giant's Causeway, also, before commencing a journey, but the great majority were issued on the cars by the conductors. The ordinary returns were available for one month, but as they were undated, in practice they were accepted for return so long as they were legible.

As there was no system of numerical stages, nor tickets for other than specified journeys, in practice (though possibly unofficially) some latitude was allowed in the limits of the journey. If a fairly regular patron boarded a car, say halfway between the Causeway and Bushmills, he would have had a good chance of being allowed to travel a similar distance beyond Bushmills, on a Giant's Causeway–Bushmills ticket.

The writer had personal experience of this about 1937, during a holiday at the Whiterocks. One afternoon, when walking along the road towards Dunluce, a Causeway bound tram, consisting of Number 9 electric car and a toast-rack trailer, overtook us about mid-way between the Whiterocks and Dunluce Castle, and we stopped it and boarded the trailer. When the conductor came for our fares we explained that we wished to get off at the Jubilee Bridge, walk the final mile along the strand and through the sandhills to the Causeway Terminus, and return thence by tram to the Whiterocks. This caused him to scratch his head, mention that there wasn't a return ticket for this sort of journey, and said we'd have to take Portrush–Giant's Causeway returns at 1s. 6d. each, and would that be all right? We agreed, and having given us our tickets, he climbed back again on to Number 9, where he sat doodling on the back of his leather cash bag for about five minutes before climbing back on to the trailer and asking for our tickets. When we had handed them over he said, 'Considerin' where ye got on, and the amount of walkin' ye're goin' to do, A think one and tuppence each would be enough', and gave us back eightpence, together with two 'Evening Excursion' tickets, which would not normally have been issued until two or three hours later.

Before the Second World War, during each summer season, ticket inspectors were stationed at Portrush depot and at Bushmills, to examine the tickets of all passengers on passing trams. At the outbreak of war these officials were transferred to other duties.

For two or three seasons before 1947 a travelling ticket inspector was employed.

Conductors' punches were similar to the railway punch of the variety which removes a portion from the edge of the ticket, the shape of the portion removed being different for each conductor's punch.

Weekly and monthly tickets were printed on stout card, blanks being left for the subscriber's name, description of journey, fare, and period of availability, which were filled in by the issuing clerk. The tickets measured 4½ in. by 3 in. and the card on which they were printed was either white, buff, or pale sage, according to category, weekly, monthly or annual, the thickness of the card increasing with the required active life of the ticket.

Journey	Single Fare Colour	Light Card Fare 1940	Light Card Fare 1949	Return Fare Colour	Heavy Card Fare 1940	Heavy Card Fare 1949
Portrush Station to Golf Club or vice versa	White	—	3d.	—	—	—
Portrush to Ballymoney Road or Giant's Causeway to Bushmills or vice versa . . .	Mauve	—	4d.	6d.	—	—	—
Portrush or Bushmills to Dunluce Castle or vice versa . .	Green	—	7d.	9d.	Lilac with Salmon band	—	10d.	1s.
Portrush to Port Ballintrae or vice versa	Buff	—	8d.	10d.	Orange with Pink band	—	1s.	1s. 3d.
Portrush to Bushmills or vice versa	Slate Blue	—	9d.	1s.	Pink	—	1s. 2d.	1s. 6d.
Portrush to Bushmills or vice versa excursion	—	—	6d.	—	One half Buff other half Salmon	—	1s.	1s. 2d.
Portrush to Giant's Causeway or vice versa . . .	Orange	—	1s.	1s. 9d.	White with Green band. Red diagonal on each half	—	1s. 6d.	3s.
Portrush to Giant's Causeway or vice versa excursion . .	—	—	—	—	One half Lilac, other half Mauve	—	1s.	1s. 6d.

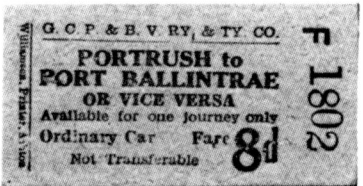

GIANT'S CAUSEWAY ELECTRIC TRAMWAY

THE WORLD'S FIRST HYDRO ELECTRIC TRAMWAY—OPENED 1883

TIME TABLE from 29th AUGUST, 1949.
UNTIL FURTHER NOTICE

Tramcars between Portrush, Bushmills and Giant's Causeway will run as follows:—

WEEK DAYS			SUNDAYS		
Portrush to Bushmills and Giant's Causeway	Giant's Causeway to Bushmills and Portrush	Bushmills to Portrush	Portrush to Bushmills and Giant's Causeway	Giant's Causeway to Bushmills and Portrush	Bushmills to Portrush
10.30 a.m.	—	8.15 a.m.	11. 0 a.m.	—	9.45 a.m.
11.20 „	—	9.45 „	12. 0 noon	—	10.45 „
12.45 p.m.	—	10.15 „	1.10 p.m.	12.15 p.m.	12.25 p.m.
2.15 „	11.20 a.m.	11.30 „	2.15 „	1. 0 „	1.10 „
3. 0 „	12.15 p.m.	12.25 p.m.	3. 0 „	2. 0 „	2.10 „
4. 5 „	1.35 „	1.45 „	4. 0 „	3. 5 „	3.15 „
5.15 „	3. 5 „	3.15 „	6. 0 „	5. 0 „	5.10 „
6. 0 „	4. 0 „	4.10 „	x7. 0 „	6. 0 „	6.10 „
7.20 „	5. 0 „	5.10 „	x8. 0 „	7. 0 „	7.10 „
x8.30 „	6.10 „	6.20 „	—	—	—
—	7.30 „	7.40 „	—	—	—

X — Bushmills only

SPECIAL EXCURSION TICKETS
Will be issued from Bushmills to Portrush Daily by all Tramcars at Fare of 1/2 Return, available for day of issue only.

SUBSCRIPTION MONTHLY AND WEEKLY TICKETS
Are issued at Reduced Rates, also Special Rates for School Children and Special Parties, on application to Tramway Office, Portrush.

Special Tramcars can be engaged on application.

Travel by Electric Tramcars, the best means of viewing the beautiful coast and enjoying the magnificent scenery.

NOTE.—This Time Table is liable to alterations, if found necessary, without notice from the Company.
The Company will not hold themselves responsible for Tramcars not starting at the times appointed, nor for delays that may occur on the road.
The Cars have special stopping places, indicated by sign, "CARS STOP HERE." Passengers are requested to meet the Cars at those places and are cautioned not to get on or off the Cars while in motion.

FARES.

	Single Fare	*Return Fare		Single Fare	*Return Fare
Portrush and Giant's Causeway	1s 9d	3s 0d	Bushmills and Dunluce Castle	9d	1s 0d
Portrush and Bushmills	1s 0d	1s 6d	Bushmills and Giant's Causeway	6d	—
Portrush and Dunluce Castle	9d	1s 0d	Portrush and White Rocks	6d	—
Portrush and Portballintrae	10d	1s 3d	Portrush and Golf Club	3d	—

*Return Tickets are available for One Month from day of issue.

G. F. MEARA, Engineer/Manager.

Portrush, 29th August, 1949.   Telephone: Portrush 2318.

The last timetable.

Appendix Seven

Sentimental Journey

A trip on the tram to the Giant's Causeway and back on a warm sunny day with good visibility was a never-to-be-forgotten pleasure, so for the benefit of those mortals unfortunate enough to have missed this experience, and also to stimulate nostalgic memories for their more fortunate fellows, let us in imagination go back to a year or so prior to the Second World War and availing ourselves of one of the 'travel bargains offered then by the Northern Counties Committee 2s. return, Belfast to Portrush Wednesday and Sunday afternoons embark on such a journey.

Our train having arrived at Portrush station, we walk along the platform towards the ticket barrier, pausing to admire the locomotive, probably a Mogul resplendent in London Midland Scottish Railway crimson lake, and named possibly *King Edward VIII, Duke of Abercorn*, or more prosaically, *Bann* or *Foyle*, which has brought us in 70 or 80 minutes from Belfast. Passing through the barrier and turning right towards the side exit to Eglinton Street, we see framed in the opening, one of the toast-rack trams. Emerging from the station, we find two rakes of trams, one headed by Saloon Motor-car Number 9 ready to start for the Causeway, and one headed by toast-rack Motor Number 20 just arrived from there.

As the day is warm, and as the small notices hanging on the dashboards of the electric cars proclaim 'Half-hour service each way' we let Number 9 depart with its rake, whilst we cross the road to purchase sweets or ice-cream at the shops opposite. Before shopping we watch the conductor remove the draw-bar between Number 20 and its trailers, and throw the bar with a clang on to the platform of the trailer. With two trailers a draw-bar was often carried at each end of the rake to avoid the conductor having to carry a bar from one end to the other. Number 20 then runs round its trailer, an operation which necessitates the policeman on point duty at the crossroads in front of the station holding up traffic as the tramway cross-over is sited in the centre of the road junction. Number 20 backs up to its trailers, the driver being at the end next the trailer, and while the driver carefully inches the car up, the conductor guides the end of the draw-bar on to the eye below the platform of Number 20 until the retaining pin drops into place. The safety-chain between the cars is hooked up, and having supervised the shunting operation, we adjourn for ice-cream, being careful, however, to return in time to ensconce ourselves in the seat behind the driver.

As the hands of the station clock move to within a few minutes of starting time, the cars fill up, and the driver and conductor emerge from the tramway office on the opposite side of the street. A lady of mature years and ample curves is experiencing some difficulty in negotiating the somewhat high and narrow footboards of a toast-rack trailer so the conductor gives her an unceremonious but friendly boost to the top step, on his way to the rear end of Number 20. The driver looks back from the front platform to see that all is well, at the same time giving the foot-gong an enquiring bang and the brake-handle an impressive whirl on its ratchet. Receiving an answering clang from the rear gong, he sets the cavalcade in motion. As we proceed at a dignified four or five miles per hour past the Town Hall and along Eglinton Street, the sides of the cars brush the shoulders of the crowds of holiday makers on the adjacent pavement and the driver keeps sounding the gong more or less sedately and at frequent intervals, a sudden imperious clang every now and then being directed at some particularly absent-minded or suicidally inclined pedestrian. At the same time, our progress is accompanied by that gritty rumble peculiar to steel wheels running on dusty steel rails. Negotiation of the Methodist Church curve into Causeway Street is accomplished only with a considerable amount of flange squeal in spite of the rail flanges having been liberally anointed with second-hand oil by a thoughtful member of the permanent way department. Having picked up a couple of passengers at the stop outside. the post office, we rumble our way along Causeway Street, speed increasing to nine or ten miles per hour as the congestion in the street eases somewhat, and the sound of the wheels changes to a more sonorous note as we leave the stone-paved track on the roadway for the unpaved path of the 'reserved' track. Passing close to the wall of the gas works we jolt first left, and then right to come to rest in the passing loop in front of the tramway depot, as the single track ahead is occupied by an incoming tram. This short pause allows tramway enthusiasts like ourselves to peer through the depot doors and attempt to see which vehicles are out of service, or to try to forecast from the quantity of rails and sleepers stacked outside, what permanent way works are envisaged for the coming winter. Non tramway enthusiasts can indulge their taste, if any, for antiquarianism by gazing on the ancient and ornate cast-iron drinking fountain, with its pillars and dome, like some miniature temple. Alternatively, they may prefer the more austere fluted column, crowned with a frame to receive, but innocent of, an oil-lamp. Neither fountain nor lamp have functioned for generations.

The incoming tram having arrived alongside, and the crews having exchanged greetings, our conductor sounds the gong and we move off again, this time along sleeper track laid apparently on the footpath, though the sleepers arc not much in evidence as the limestone ballast had been generously applied to well above sleeper height, and subsequently has been levelled to a more or less continuous surface by the passage of many feet, so that the track appears as two brown lines on a white path, embellished with frequent tufts of grass, buttercups or daisies, which add a touch of colour.

On leaving the depot, our speed has risen to a respectable 15 or 16 miles per hour, and the lightly-sprung cars jiggle about intriguingly to the characteristic, and not unpleasant, clack-clack of the wheels passing over the joints of the 20 ft rails, the whine of the motor gears and the jingle-jangle of the safety chains providing a continuous musical background as we pass Holyrood Hotel and commence the climb to the Whiterocks. On our left we look across the golf links, where devotees of the 'Royal and Ancient' are 'skelping the gutty', to the sand-hills hiding the East Strand, from which the salty tang of the sea assails our nostrils. Our progress remains brisk through the first passing-loop half-a-mile from the depot, but halfway up the steeper gradient beyond the loop, speed suddenly begins to fall, though the driver has not moved his controller from the full-speed position. As our speed continues to drop until it is little, if any, more than that of a slow walk, the waggish passengers commence to crack the usual jokes, and the uninitiated become somewhat apprehensive at the thought of having to walk. However, the seasoned travellers know that the diminished speed is only due to a couple of other cars somewhere along the line, starting up gradients, thus creating a demand for current which taxes the generators to their capacity. As one of these unseen cars tops its hill, speed rises again and we arrive safely at the Whiterocks passing-loop and stopping point, where some passengers leave the cars. At the corner just beyond the passing-loop we see the hut of one of the flagmen and as the white flag flying indicates that he has given the road beyond to a Portrush-bound tram, we wait in the loop until this appears, meanwhile enjoying the bird's-eye view of the incomparable stretch of golden strand dotted with the tiny figures of children in gay colours, and backed by the grassy sandhills with their quota of romantic courting couples. Seawards, about a mile off-shore across a stretch of blue water, the long line of rocky islands known as the Skerries rises like some breakwater against the ocean swell. The incoming tram having passed, the flag-man substitutes a red flag, thus blocking the road to any incoming car, and we proceed past his hut to drop down the grade past the limestone quarry which rejoices in the name of 'Long Gilbert' and into which the only industrial siding of the tramway had been laid in February 1883. All trace of the siding has long since disappeared, but a 3ft gauge incline worked by a petrol-engine-powered winch still exists (1939) to bring the limestone from the quarry floor up to road level where it is loaded into road vehicles for distribution.

Beyond the quarry, the road swings to the right and then sharply to the left, around the steep cleft in the rock known as the Devil's Punchbowl. As the tram rounds this curve, the wheel flanges groan and screech in protest against the check-rails, and passengers on the sea-ward side of the cars can look almost vertically down to the water which even on the calmest day churns incessantly among the rocks below, and which is consequently always covered by a heaving mass of froth. With an on-shore gale blowing, the cleft is an inferno of tumbling water, and the wind causes spray and foam to shoot up the narrow funnel and shower the roadway, as though the Devil himself were lashing his punch around in a frenzy of demoniacal rage.

On rounding the Punchbowl we climb fairly steeply through a passing-loop and along the top of the cliffs, with excellent views of the massive limestone rock formations known as the Giant's Head with its ridiculously small black basalt crown; the Wishing Arch which somehow always suggested to the writer a broadside view of an elephant; and the Lion's Paw a long, narrow peninsula of rock stretching out into the sea.

The sea here is remarkably clear and as passengers in the tram looked into it at an angle of 45° or so, it was quite possible to see any reasonably-sized sea animal, such as a basking shark or a seal, swimming under the surface. The writer well remembers watching on several occasions schools of porpoises demonstrating their brand of aquabatics as he passed along this stretch of coast on the tram. If the display were good, the driver would obligingly slow down to afford the passengers an uninterrupted view of the performance.

During the war an additional, 'though more sinister, display was provided here by the Allied air forces as this piece of sea was used as a practice ground for submarine spotting, bombing, etc.

Continuing round the reverse curves, we reach the next passing-loop adjacent to Clooney Hill, the summit of the line and 190 ft. above sea-level. Looking backwards from this vantage point, we can see the white cliffs around which we have just passed, and the long line of the Whiterocks Strand stretching away to terminate in the rocky eminence of Ramore Head, topped with its coast guard look-out and signal mast, and surrounded by the houses of Portrush. A plume of white steam tells of a departing train and behind all, the dark blue mountains of the Inishowen peninsula rise like a backcloth beyond Lough Foyle.

To the north, the ocean stretches uninterruptedly to the horizon where two apparently independent islands can be seen. Actually they are both part of Islay, some 30 miles away, and given the correct atmospheric conditions the low-lying ground between can be seen, as also can the Paps of Jura rising behind the Islay skyline.

Topping the summit, and rounding a bend on the road, the ruins of Dunluce Castle perched high above the sea on the edge of a precipitous cliff, swing into view somewhat below us and to our left, as our driver shuts off power and applies the brakes to check our speed on the descent to Dunluce crossing. The gradient is steep and ends in a sharp bend and a road crossing, so the conductor reaches back over the rear dashboard of the motor-car and screws down the brakes on the first trailer, otherwise the effect of gravity on the two trailers might be more than the adhesion of the motorcar could hold in check.

The conductor gives three deliberate clangs on his foot-gong, the signal to the driver that passengers wish to alight, and we roll to a stop just clear of the road leading to the Castle. Having disgorged a number of hikers with their rucksacks, and the conductor having released the trailer brakes, we roll on through the passing-loop, noting the crude sentry-box-like erection containing the equipment for dividing the tramway into two sections electrically.

A red flag flying at the Gallery indicates that the flag-man there has given us the road and we continue through the loop and on to the sharp bend of the Gallery, from which we can look almost vertically down to the waves breaking on the rocky shore, having passed the minute area between the boundary wall and the cliff edge on which the flag-man's hut is perched in a manner somewhat reminiscent of Mahomet's coffin.

Rounding the Gallery, we gain speed on a descending gradient, but as we approach the next corner, a Portrush-bound tram is stopped and reversed 50 yards or so to the passing-loop at the point where the coast road to Portballintrae branches to the left. Such a contretemps at this point is by no means unusual, as the driver of a tram from the Causeway has to run through this loop before he can see the flag at the Gallery.

As we follow the reversing tram, its conductor emerges from the boskage of the track-side hedge into which he has had to compress himself to clear the sides of the vehicles of his caravanserie, whilst he held up the weighted point-lever to let the vehicles reverse into the proper road. Deprived of the conductor's support, the lever restores the points to their normal position and our tram enters the passing-loop and stops to allow some passengers to alight for the small fishing village of Portballintrae which has come into view as a line of cottages and summer residences, straggling along the edge of a small strand half-a-mile or so away below us on our left. Leaving the passing-loop we cross the end of the coast road with a rumble of wheels and pick up speed to 15 miles an hour or so on the down grade to Gortnee siding or passing-loop, where we stop again to set down some other visitors for Portballintrae who prefer the 'Port Hedge' field path to the county road for their walk to the village. On receiving the conductor's all-clear, the driver puts on power and we move out of the loop and on to a steady down-grade which continues for a mile into Bushmills. Having cleared the loop, the driver switches off power, the conductor hauls the trolley down from the overhead wire and anchors it under the hook provided for the purpose at either end of the roof of the motor-car, and we proceed to coast at 15 or 20 miles per hour down the long grade to Bushmills. To a thrifty outfit like the Giant's Causeway Tramway Company, the expense of providing a hook at each end of the car roof was money well spent in view of the saving in wear and tear of trolley wheels and overhead wires, as about five miles of coasting was possible on each complete return journey of 16 miles.

Coasting down from Gortnee Siding, we see in front of us a line of low hills, softly green and gently rounded, which form the horizon a mile or so away on the other side of the Bush Valley. Unlike most of the high ground in the locality, these hills are pleasantly covered with small copses of trees, interspersed with pasture land, for they are part of Dundarave Estate, the seat of the Macnaghten family, between whom and the tramway company, relations at times became somewhat strained. According to local tradition, the copses of trees represent the relative positions of the various detachments of troops at the battle of Waterloo, having been planted thus soon after that event by the Macnaghten of the period.

Soon the conical roof and clock on the tower of Bushmills Market House rise above the hedges in front of us as our driver sounds his gong and takes up the slack in his brakes on approaching some cottages around which children are playing, and dogs and hens scurry to and fro. Passing these cottages, and running through the passing-loop known as Stanalane Siding, in two or three minutes we bounce over the points and grind round a sharp left-hand curve to come to rest in front of Bushmills station house, from which emerges an official with uniform cap bearing the legend 'Electric Tramway', similar to those worn by our own driver and conductor. This is the ticket inspector who, having collected the tickets of travellers leaving the cars, then proceeds to examine those of the passengers remaining in their seats. A minute or two completes this ceremony, and he gives the driver the right away. The trolley having been reintroduced to the overhead wire by the conductor during the ticket inspection, the driver gives the motors a couple of notches of the controller, and to the sound of the foot-gong we slowly pass the remains of the water tank and erstwhile crossing gate, and cautiously cross the Bushmills–Portballintrae road to enter the private right-of-way of the Causeway extension.

On our left rises a steep grassy bank, whilst on the right the ground falls away for a hundred yards or so to the River Bush meandering placidly in great loops through the meadows below, from the grey stonework of the Bush Bridge and the houses of the little town on the right, the woods of Dundarave and Bushmills Braes rising behind to the skyline.

In about half-a-mile the tramway changes course to the right by 60° to run almost due north along the river first through fields and then through Bushfoot Golf Links, where a small, red-painted corrugated-iron shelter with name board graces the stopping place provided for the convenience of golfers.

A quarter-of-a-mile farther on we veer slightly to the left on a high embankment and rumble across the Victoria Jubilee Bridge over the brown peaty waters of the Bush 25 ft below, in which the sun's rays may catch the silvery glint of a salmon gliding majestically. Beyond the bridge the line enters the sandhills and rabbit warren through which it passes for four or five hundred yards before coming out on the Bushfoot Strand where a passing-loop and stopping-point have been located. To the left the rocky outline of Runkerry Point rises from the sea with the buildings of Runkerry House ranged along its base apparently just above sea-level, like some animal crouching in shelter from the wind.

Here we pause to unload a couple of family parties prepared for a jolly afternoon on the beach, complete with buckets and spades, and bottles of fizzy lemonade. Resuming our journey, we pass through a wide cutting in the sandhills, and through Runkerry passing-loop before curving to the right and commencing a 1 in 40 climb, during which speed drops to walking pace, before we clatter through the catch point and come to rest in the Causeway Terminus.

While the passengers are disembarking, the conductor is screwing down the hand-brakes on the trailers, then, seeing some elderly passenger experiencing difficulty in negotiating the narrow and steep footboards of a toast-rack, he goes to their assistance before uncoupling the motor-car ready for its run round the trailers. As Number 9 and its train have been parked on the long track beyond the run-round loop for return on a later service, and as Number 23 with its trailers are lined up on the passing-loop for departure in five or ten minutes, Number 20 cannot run round until 23 departs, so the conductor can only reverse the seat backs in the meantime.

As we have already gazed upon the geological wonders of the Giant's Causeway, we change over to a couple of vacant seats on one of Number 23's trailers for a more or less immediate departure for Portrush.

The appointed time having arrived, and everyone being safely on board, the conductor mounts the lowest footboard at the driver's end and the cars move off. Approaching the station limits, he drops off and runs ahead to throw the catch-point into the closed position and hold it there till the last trailer has passed. The driver stops the cars until the conductor is safely on board the first trailer and then lets them roll again by gravity, the conductor having hooked down the trolley from the trailer, on which he remains to manipulate the hand-brake during the descent of Giveen's Bank, as the steep incline between the Causeway and Runkerry Siding is known.

The bank having been negotiated safely, the conductor releases the trailer brake, restores the trolley to the overhead wire whilst on the move, and commences his somewhat precarious pilgrimage along the foot-boards to check and issue tickets, while we proceed at a good speed along the sandhills. The right of way here conveys the impression of being along a wide green carpet as the springy grass is kept cropped short by the sheep that wander among the dunes in considerable numbers. The grassy turf softens the harsher noises of the cars, and makes our progress very pleasant and restful, the only break being the rumble across the Jubilee Bridge.

As we approach the last passing-loop before Bushmills, we see a tram waiting therein, and as we get nearer, it is obvious that something unusual is happening as most of its passengers are out on the track. Coming alongside we learn that the second trailer has derailed on the points and as many male passengers as can get a hold on it are lifting it back on to the rails. We are informed that this is the second time it has derailed on its journey from Portrush, but most of the passengers consider that this has only added to the enjoyment and has provided them with material for an unlimited number of funny and libellous stories about 'the Tram'.

As the crew and occupants appear to have the matter well under control, we resume our journey, observing as we glance back, that the refractory trailer is Number 13. Later discreet enquiries among friendly members of the tramway staff elicited the fact that Number 13 had been out of service some time awaiting the fitting of new wheels, as the old flanges were worn thin, but due to a sudden rush of traffic it had had to be pressed into service.

After leaving Number 13, our journey onwards to Portrush is uneventful, apart from a spirited run down from the Whiterocks to Portrush depot for the benefit of a couple of passengers wishing to catch a train, and who had missed the bus they intended to take into Portrush. Such an effort called for considerable concentration on braking by both driver and conductor, as the latter had to manipulate the trailer brakes in co-operation with the former, to avoid the possibility of the trailers 'jack-knifing' when the brakes on the motor-car were applied.

However, we reach the depot safely and by good luck the outgoing tram is waiting for us in the loop so that we can proceed without delay up Causeway Street, though of necessity our progress here is by no means spectacular, due to the presence of other road users, as we are running on the wrong side of the road. Luckily, there are no vehicles parked on the track, and we reach the railway station in time for our two passengers to catch their train. Our driver and conductor relax once again, as along with the remainder of the passengers we de-tram and set off down the street in search of tea.

Appendix Eight

Mr W. A. Traill

William Atcheson Traill was born in 1844, the third son of William Traill, Esq., Ballylough House, Bushmills, Co. Antrim.

He graduated at Trinity College, Dublin, in 1865, and took the degree of M.A.Ing. (Master of Engineering) in 1873.

For some time, Mr Traill was employed on HM Geological Survey of Ireland, and was a strong protagonist of the use of boreholes for water supplies, where possible.

His interest in electric traction having been aroused in connection with the Giant's Causeway Tramway, and following the experiments in this sphere carried out on that line between 1881 and 1883, Mr Traill was granted Patents Nos. 3275 and 3277 on 2nd July, 1883. The first of these was for 'improvements to the side-contact system of current collection to avoid damage to the collector due to travelling in alternate directions, also to avoid liability of passers-by receiving accidental shocks from the conductor'. The second was for a system of current collection in which the 'conductor should be enclosed in an iron tube laid below ground between the running rails, the tube being provided with a longitudinal slot through which one or more collector arms projecting from the carriage might travel in contact with the conductor'.

W.A. Traill, M.A.Ing

The latter patent, which was the genesis of the system applied years after to the London County Council Tramways and others, was sold by Mr Traill to an American buyer, for a small sum.

Another transport undertaking with which Mr Traill was connected was the Liverpool Overhead Railway. Proposals for an elevated line along the docks at Liverpool were considered spasmodically from about 1852, and eventually, in 1888, the Act incorporating the Liverpool Overhead Railway was obtained, and construction commenced in 1889.

The campaign for this overhead railway had not passed unnoticed by Mr Traill, and, when a reasonable degree of success with electric traction had been achieved on the Giant's Causeway Tramway, he worked out a scheme for a double-tracked electric line carried on a viaduct above the existing Mersey Docks & Harbour Board Railway serving the docks.

His design incorporated the side-contact system then in use on the Giant's Causeway Tramway, and for a double-tracked line two live rails would, of course, have been necessary. These Mr Traill proposed to locate in the 'six-foot' way between the tracks, together with the feeder cables, the latter to be protected from accidental damage and the weather in a covered duct.

To illustrate his proposals, Mr Traill had made for him a working model, to a scale of 1 in. to 1 ft which he exhibited at the International Inventions Exhibition held in London in 1885. This so impressed the International Committee of Judges that they awarded him a Silver Medal for Tramways. The model was 28 ft long and comprised a timber deck supported on pillars and lattice girders, these components being properly proportioned and beautifully cast, the pillars in iron, and the girders in phosphor bronze.

This viaduct supported a double-tracked electric railway on which ran a working model of a Giant's Causeway saloon motor-car. This car had been exhibited previously at the meeting of the British Association at Montreal in 1884, to illustrate a paper on 'The Pioneer Hydro-electric Tramway of the World', and so must be one of the oldest, if not actually the oldest, working model of an electric tramcar in the world.

Under the viaduct, a double-tracked railway, complete with goods wagons, was arranged to represent the Mersey Docks and Harbour Board line.

In July 1933, the Golden Jubilee Year of the Giant's Causeway Tramway, and just a year before his death, Mr Traill presented this model to the Belfast Municipal Museum and Art Gallery. Due to limitation of space, only half of the length of viaduct could be accepted, together with the car and trucks, and the remaining half of the viaduct went to the Hull Museum.

When checking over some rolls of drawings and maps from the Giant's Causeway line, the writer noticed what appeared to be a faint pencil 'doodle' on the back of an old Ordnance Sheet. Closer investigation revealed it to be a sketch of Mr Traill's proposal for the Liverpool Overhead Railway, presumably drawn by himself.

The pillars, girders, etc., of the model follow closely those shown on the sketch, which also shows clearly the position of the conductor rails and feeder cables between the tracks. The cars on the overhead track are obviously based on the closed and open motor-cars of the Giant's Causeway Tramway.

Reverting to the Liverpool Overhead Railway, in the event Mr Traill's proposals were not adopted, at any rate in detail, as for the first few years of operation the live rail was located centrally between the running rails of each track, though it is interesting to note that the electrification of the Liverpool Overhead Railway. was carried out by the Electric Construction Co., the firm which, as Elwell Parker Ltd., had supplied the generator for Walkmills Power Station in 1887, and later supplied other generators to the Giant's Causeway Tramway in 1900 and 1907.

Some years after the opening, the Liverpool Overhead Railway and the Lancashire & Yorkshire Railway decided that it would be advantageous to both if through running of trains between their respective lines were possible, and to permit Lancashire & Yorkshire Railway rolling-stock to operate on the Liverpool Overhead Railway, conductor rails were provided in the 'six-foot' way on the latter line, almost in the exact position suggested some ten years earlier by Mr Traill.

Rough sketch believed to be by Mr. Traill of his plan for the Liverpool Overhead Railway, showing Giant's Causeway type cars on the upper level with side collectors.

An early photograph, before the overhead system was constructed, of motor-car No. 4 and trailer No. 10 passing Dunluce Castle. *Oakwood collection*

INDEX

Accidents, 29, 41, 42, 48, 55, 58, 67, 69, 70, 76, 78, 79
Alexander & Sons, 70
Antrim County Council, 53, 70, 82
Antrim Electricity Distribution Co., 69
Armstrong, Major, 32
Attempts to sell tramway, 48, 58, 64, 80, 82
Auction of tramway assets, 83
Ballycastle Railway, 7, 9, 10, 66
Ballymena, 7, 65
Ballymena and Larne Railway, 7, 12
Ballymena, Cushendall and Red Bay Railway, 7, 10
Bann Breakwater, 67
Bann Navigation, 81
Bann River, 67
Belfast, 7, 59, 60, 74, 111
Belfast & Northern Counties Railway, 7, 10, 15, 48; exchange siding, 24, 28; Harbour Branch, , 15, 24, 38, 52; opposition , 12; relations, 33, 47
Belfast Corporation Tramways, 75
Belfast Corporation Transport, 78
Bessbrook and Newry Tramway, 80
Beyer, Peacock & Co., 43
Black Rock Strand, 26, 28, 41
Board of Trade inspection, 16, 27, 32
Board of Works, 53
Bramwell, Sir Frederick, 31
Brittish Griffin Chilled Iron & Steel Co., 59
Bruce, Sir Hervey, 19
Bush River, 10, 16, 27, 35, 53, 60, 77, 80, 81, 115
Bushmills, 7, 13, 19, 103, 114; Market Yard, 15, 27, 115; Coleraine Road, 27, 99; Portballintrae Road, 27, 35; proposed railways, 9, 11; Square, 27; Station, 31, 34, 35, 42, 48, 55, 115; Supplying electricity to, 60; Tram sheds, 29, 41, 49, 77
Cardew, Major, 42, 101
Carrick-a-Rede, 49, 57
Causeway Hotel, 19, 29, 30, 40, 67
Chaine, James, 12
Chamberlain & Hookham, 57
Chambers, William, 65, 68, 69, 70, 81
Clooney Hill, 27, 58, 81, 113
Cloughmills, 10
Clutha Ironworks, 36
Coal; Traffic, 28; Deposits, 7
Company receipts, 21, 41, 56, 59, 63, 65, 66, 68, 72, 74, 79, 81, 82
Competition; Charabanc, 49, 57, 59, 65; Motor bus, 66, 67
Construction cost, 31
Cork, Bandon & South Coast Railway, 56
Dervock to Giant's Causeway proposed railway, 10, 11, 12, 22, 30
Devil's Punch Bowl, 27, 113
Dundrave, 11, 114
Dunfermline and District Tramway, 70, 94
Dunluce, 18, 103
Dunluce Castle, 1, 27, 113
Dunluce Mines, 48
Dynamo, 13, 19
Electric Construction Co., 45, 49, 60, 101
Electric traction, 13, 14, 18, 33, 38, 43, 60, 73; Collecting brushes, 15; Conductor rail, 14, 15, 16, 26; Jubilee Commemoration, 67, 68; Overhead Wires, 44, 45, 56, 56, 69, 77, 103-104; Power cable, 27, 39; power loss, 14, 15, 22; Three rail system, 13; Two rail system, 13, 14

INDEX

Electricity Board for Northern Ireland, 76
English Electric Co., 59
Fall, David, 55
Fielding & Platt, 53
First sod cut, 13
Fisher, Mr, 7
Fitzgerald, Mrs, 28
Flag Man, Gallery Hill, 46, 47
General Strike, 65
Geoghegan Patent tipping wagon, 16, 92
Geoghegan, Mr, 16
Geological Surbvey of Ireland, 9
Giant's Causeway, 7, 10, 11, 115; Extension, 30, 31, 34, 35-40, 115; Terminus, 36, 37, 47, 81, 103, 115; Tourist traffic, 11, 22, 28, 57, 63, 65, 74
Giant's Causeway Columnar Basalt Co., 50
Goods rates, 28, 39
Gortnee Siding, 38, 39, 55, 114
Government control, 55, 47
Grand Jury, 9, 13, 18, 28
Great Northern Railway, 66
Guinness Brewery, 16
High Sheriff of County Antrim, 21, 31
Holden Train, 48
Hopkins, Dr., 19
Hopkinson, Dr. Edward, 13, 88, 103
Hutchinson, Major General, 16, 32
Hydro-electric power, 13
Incidents; Electric locomotive hauls steam one, 18; Blizzards, 56, 77; Doctor encourages shock therapy, 32; Drifting barrage balloon, 78; Naval bombardment, 55; Power leak at opening ceremony, 22
Iron; deposits, 7, 11, 28; mining, 7, 33
Isle of Man Railway, 7
Keenan, Michael, 65, 68, 69
Larne, 10
Lichterfield, Germany, 13
Limestone, 11, 28, 39, 113
Lissanoure, 10
Livery, 71, 77, 92
London, Midland & Scottish Railway, 58
Long Gilbert Quarry, 26, 113
Longfield, Judge, 13
Lord Kelvin, 13, 21, 31, 32
Lord Lieutenant of Ireland, Earl Spencer, 16, 20, 21, 22
Macnaghten, Sir W. T., 11, 48, 114
Malleable Steel Casting Co., 49, 92
Maxwell, Robert, 64, 68, 102
McCurdy, Mr, 60, 61, 65
Meera, G.F., 81, 82
Midland Carriage Co., 16
Midland Railway, 48
Mineral resources, development, 9
Ministry of Labour, 66
Moon, Howard, 29
National Gas Engine Co., 60, 85, 86
Northern Counties Committee, 48, 49, 58, 59, 60, 64, 65, 66, 67, 68
Opening ceremony, 19, 20
Orblereagh Mines, 18, 28
Passenger fares, 18, 28, 57, 59, 66, 67, 68, 78, 79, 107-109; Numbers, 37, 56, 57, 68, 69
Passing loop, 12, 26, 73; Devil's Punch Bowl, 38; Dunluce, 12, 46, 113; Giant's Head, 41; Portballintrae Road, 35, 46, 70; Whiterocks, 12, 26
Portballintrae, 23, 27, 41, 114
Portrush; Ballymoney Road, 26, 28, 61; Causeway Street, 26, 39, 52, 58,112; Croc-na-Mac Road, 52; Depot, 15, 16, 19, 20, 23, 26, 39, 57, 69, 70, 72, 76, 83, 103, 105, 112, 116; Distillery, 39; Dunluce Street, 52; Eglinton Street, 12, 24, 39, 50, 52, 71, 74, 111, 116; Gas Works, 50, 71; Harbour, 50; Kerr Street, 24; Lifeboat, 41; Main Street, 12; Mark Street, 24; Methodist Church curve, 24, 45, 70, 71, 112; Power station, 16, 18, 19, 41, 53, 55, 60, 61, 63, 64, 80; Station, 6, 15, 19, 23, 38, 39, 55, 65, 70,111; Town Hall, 24, 111
Portrush & Bushmills Tramway, 11, 12
Portrush Harbour Tramway Co., 28, 33, 39
Portrush Urban District Council, 45, 53, 55, 82
Post-war Irish Railway Compensation , 57
Public meetings, 13
Quarries, 26, 28, 50, 53, 67, 113
Queen Victoria, 19, 26
Rathkenny, 10
Red Cross, 74
Road Transport Board, 70
Rolling Stock, 27, 28, 29, 34, 38, 39, 41, 46, 47, 49, 50, 87-98
Royal Irish Constabulary, 20
Runkerry Siding, 81, 115
Sandhills Siding, 81
Scott, Robert, 51, 58, 64, 68, 97
Siemens, 13, 14, 19, 27, 29, 67, 88, 100, 101
Siemens, Dr. William, 13
Siemens, Sir Chas., 31
Sinclair, W., 64
Society of Arts, London, 19, 88
Steam working, 16, 18, 24, 38, 39, 43, 47, 55, 63; Bog-wood for fuel, 63
Sunday Trams, 28
Switzerland, 37
Tate, Mr, 16
Telephone lines, 21, 47, 49, 77, 103
Thompson, Sir William (see Lord Kelvin),
Toonerville Trolley, 74
Track raising, 58, 66, 70
Traffic, Goods, 16, 28, 38, 48
Traffic, Mail, 38
Traill, Dr. Anthony, 9, 13, 21, 31, 55
Traill, W. A. Mrs, 13
Traill. William Atcheson, 9, 11, 13, 16, 18, 20, 22, 32, 41, 44, 50, 55, 56, 59, 67, 117-118; call for resignation, 60; death, 68
Tram Improvements; Condensor units fitted, 72; Electric heaters fitted, 74, 75; Glazed ends fitted, 76, 77; Goods wagons converted, 39, 41; Head lamps, 67; Roofs added, 70; Tramcar meter, , 57
Trinity College, Dublin, 13, 31
Ulster Steam Tram Company, 9, 12
Ulster Tourist Board, 82
Ulster Transport Authority, 80
United States Armed Forces, 74
Victoria Jubilee Bridge, 35, 36, 81, 86, 97, 115
Vignoles, Mr, 7
Walkmills hydro-electric power station, 16, 18, 19, 21, 27, 47, 61, 64, 67, 80, 99-102; Dynamo, 27, 45, 100; Generator, 37, 49, 60, 66, 103; Turbine, 27, 45, 48, 77, 81
War Department, claim on, 78
Water rights, 16, 53, 56
Water shortage, 53, 61, 77, 80
Water Tanks, 86
White, William, 29, 61
Whiterocks, 18, 26, 28, 70, 103, 112, 113, 116
Wier Bros., 57
Wilkinson & Co. , 16, 33, 43, 85, 87
Winter closure, 63, 65
Winter service resumes, 73